WRITING SPACES: READINGS ON WRITING 3

Writing Spaces: Readings on Writing

Editors

Dana Driscoll, Indiana University of Pennsylvania
Mary Stewart, Indiana University of Pennsylvania
Matthew Vetter, Indiana University of Pennsylvania

Copyeditors

Ashley Cerku, Oakland University
Brynn Fitzsimmons, University of Kansas
Megan Heise, Indiana University of Pennsylvania
Jennifer Johnson, University of California, Santa Barbara
Heather A. McDonald, American University
John Whicker, Fontbonne University

Web Editor

Joshua Daniel-Wariya, Oklahoma State University

Social Media Editor

Delilah Pope

Volumes in *Writing Spaces: Readings on Writing* offer multiple perspectives on a wide range of topics about writing. In each chapter, authors present their unique views, insights, and strategies for writing by addressing the undergraduate reader directly. Drawing on their own experiences, these teachers-as-writers invite students to join in the larger conversation about the craft of writing. Consequently, each essay functions as a standalone text that can easily complement other selected readings in first year writing or writing-intensive courses across the disciplines at any level.

All volumes in the series are published under a Creative Commons license and available for download at the Writing Spaces website (http://www.writingspaces.org), Parlor Press (http://www.parlorpress.com/writingspaces), and the WAC Clearinghouse (http://wac.colostate.edu/).

WRITING SPACES

Readings on Writing
Volume 3

Edited by Dana Driscoll, Mary Stewart
and Matthew Vetter

Parlor Press
Anderson, South Carolina
www.parlorpress.com

Parlor Press LLC, Anderson, South Carolina, USA

© 2021 by Parlor Press. Individual essays © 2021 by the respective authors. Unless otherwise stated, these works are licensed under the Creative Commons Attribution-NonCommercial-NoDerivatives 4.0 International License (CC BY-NC-ND 4.0) and are subject to the Writing Spaces Terms of Use. To view a copy of this license, visit http://creativecommons.org/licenses/by-nc-nd/4.0/, email info@creativecommons.org, or send a letter to Creative Commons, PO Box 1866, Mountain View, CA 94042, USA. To view the Writing Spaces Terms of Use, visit http://writingspaces.org/terms-of-use.

All rights reserved.
Printed in the United States of America

S A N: 2 5 4 - 8 8 7 9

Library of Congress Cataloging-in-Publication Data

Writing spaces : readings on writing. Volume 1 / edited by Charles Lowe and Pavel Zemliansky.
   p. cm.
Includes bibliographical references and index.
ISBN 978-1-60235-184-4 (pbk. : alk. paper) -- ISBN 978-1-60235-185-1 (adobe ebook)
1. College readers. 2. English language--Rhetoric. I. Lowe, Charles, 1965- II. Zemliansky, Pavel.
PE1417.W735 2010
808'.0427--dc22

2010019487

2 3 4 5

978-1-64317-127-2 (paperback)
978-1-64317-128-9 (pdf)
978-1-64317-129-6 (epub)

Cover design by Colin Charlton.
Printed on acid-free paper.

Parlor Press, LLC is an independent publisher of scholarly and trade titles in print and multimedia formats. This book is available in paper, and eBook formats from Parlor Press on the World Wide Web at http://www.parlorpress.com or through online and brick-and-mortar bookstores. It is also available in eBook formats at http://writingspaces.org and http://wac.colostate.edu/. For submission information or to find out about Parlor Press publications, write to Parlor Press, 3015 Brackenberry Drive, Anderson, South Carolina, 29621, or email editor@parlorpress.com.

Contents

1 Punctuation's Rhetorical Effects   *3*
   Kevin Cassell

2 Understanding Visual Rhetoric   *18*
   Jenae Cohn

3 How to Write Meaningful Peer Response Praise   *40*
   Ron DePeter

4 Writing with Force and Flair   *52*
   William T. FitzGerald

5 An Introduction to and Strategies for Multimodal Composing   *65*
   Melanie Gagich

6 Grammar, Rhetoric, and Style   *86*
   Craig Hulst

7 Understanding Discourse Communities   *100*
   Dan Melzer

8 The Evolution of Imitation: Building Your Style   *116*
   Craig A. Meyer

9 Constructing Scholarly Ethos in the Writing Classroom   *128*
   Kathleen J. Ryan

10 Writing in Global Contexts: Composing Usable Texts for Audiences from Different Cultures   *147*
   Kirk St.Amant

11 Weaving Personal Experience into Academic Writing   *162*
   Marjorie Stewart

12 Exigency: What Makes My Message
   Indispensable to My Reader   *175*
   Quentin Vieregge

13 Assessing Source Credibility for Crafting a
   Well-Informed Argument   *189*
   Kate Warrington, Natasha Kovalyova, and Cindy King

Contributors   *205*

About the Editors   *209*

Writing Spaces: Readings on Writing 3

1 Punctuation's Rhetorical Effects

Kevin Cassell

Overview

Many students tend to think of punctuation as governed by a set of rules. This chapter encourages them to conceive of punctuation as a system of conventions, which includes standard expectations of correct usage—certain "rules"—but applies them within a broader rhetorical context. After distinguishing between punctuation and grammar (the two terms are often associated), students are provided with three reading strategies to help them become aware of how punctuation operates in printed texts. The first strategy, explicit reading, adopts *Writing Spaces* author Mike Bunn's Reading Like a Writer (RLW) approach, but emphasizes a reading style that is sensory. The second strategy, visual reading, asks students to adopt a "typographical perspective" when reading so that they literally *see* how punctuation operates. The third one, aural reading, asks them to *listen* – possibly by reading aloud – to how punctuation conveys an author's tone of voice, which can help to illustrate context. Palpably experiencing punctuation usage while reading will help students use it with confidence and facility in their own writing.

This chapter accommodates readers with hearing or visual impairments so they may participate in this sensory reading.

I recently shared a few short written expressions with students in my first-year writing class at the University of Arizona.* Each one was a sentence or two long and conveyed a different idea that related to language use. I didn't tell my students who wrote them. I just projected

---

* This work is licensed under the Creative Commons Attribution-NonCommercial-NoDerivatives 4.0 International License (CC BY-NC-ND 4.0) and are subject to the Writing Spaces Terms of Use. To view a copy of this license, visit http://creativecommons.org/licenses/by-nc-nd/4.0/, email info@creativecommons.org, or send a letter to Creative Commons, PO Box 1866, Mountain View, CA 94042, USA. To view the Writing Spaces Terms of Use, visit http://writingspaces.org/terms-of-use.

each one on the classroom screen and asked them what they thought. They responded to the ideas of each quite well– until I put this final one up for them to read:

> Alway's; use the proper name, for thing's. Fear, of a name increase's fear, of the thing, itself.

Not a single student engaged with the *idea* here – that the way something's named can cause people to have an emotional response to it. Instead, they severely critiqued the writing itself. As I had expected, they said the writer had "bad," "clumsy," even "horrible" grammar. When I asked for examples of this bad grammar, they said the apostrophes were wrong, the semicolon didn't belong there, and there were too many incorrectly placed commas. I completely agreed with the problems they pointed out – except one.

If you ignore the apostrophes, the semicolon, and the commas, then you'll see that the *grammar* of this two-sentence expression is fine. In fact, the original version had none of those punctuation marks. I put them there after taking it from one of the most popular books in the world – J. K. Rowling's *Harry Potter and the Sorcerer's Stone*. If you've read this book, you may remember the half-blood wizard Professor Dumbledore explaining to young Harry why he calls the villainous Voldermort by his real name and not "the Dark Lord" or "He-Who-Must-Not-Be-Named," which are terms that undeservedly inflate his status to mythic proportions (298). Here are the actual two sentences before I got my hands on them:

> Always use the proper name for things. Fear of a name increases fear of the thing itself.

I incorrectly punctuated these sentences to demonstrate two things. First, I want to point out that there is a difference between grammar and punctuation. Grammar refers to the structure of sentences. If I had changed the *grammar* of the first sentence, it would have come out as *The proper name for things always use* or, worse, *Things the proper name always use for.* Instead, I just added a number of punctuation marks in places where they didn't belong, which demonstrates my second point: nonstandard use of punctuation not only can confuse or distract readers, it gives them the impression that you can't write well, that you have "bad grammar" even though your sentences may be grammatically sound.

Many of us automatically connect the words *grammar* and *punctuation* because we tend to think of them together. Why is that? I think it goes back to our early school days when we first started to learn how to write in English. We learned that we couldn't arbitrarily string phrases into sentences and sentences into paragraphs on a whim. There were "rules" to follow—and if we didn't follow the rules, our papers would come back scrawled upon with lots of marks we couldn't comprehend.

Let's talk for a moment about these "rules." You may be surprised to know that many writing instructors, including me, are uncomfortable with this term because it sounds so fixed and rigid. We know that language is fluid and changes when we use it in different situations. Therefore, instead of "rules," we prefer to use the more flexible word *conventions*, which includes standard expectations of correct usage—certain "rules"—but applies them within a broader context in which authors frequently have options on how and when to use punctuation. In other words, we need to use punctuation effectively, not *just* correctly.

This chapter isn't going to teach you the right and wrong ways to use punctuation marks. Instead, it's going to make explicit things we already *know* about punctuation so that we can understand it better and use it with expression and facility. I just punctuated the word "know" using *italics*[1] to stress that, yes, we are all pretty familiar with punctuation simply through our ongoing exposure to written English. All learners of English implicitly acquire this familiarity by reading books, social media posts, posters, road signs, recipes, and even the privacy policies of software products that we download to our computers (yeah, right!). Still, many of us – including native English speakers – need to explicitly learn how punctuation operates. One way to do that is to consult the handbooks and online tutorials where we can read about the standard usage expectations – including "rules" – of punctuation and see correct examples. But there are other ways to learn about punctuation that are not beholden to rules, and this essay is going to show you a couple of them. All you need are these pages you're reading now and a perceptive reading style that another *Writing Spaces* author, Mike Bunn, calls RLW – "Reading Like a Writer." In order to help you understand how punctuation operates in written English, I'm going to ask you to adopt an RLW approach that is *sensory* – that is, I want you to both *see* and *hear* how punctuation operates on whatever page you're reading, including this one. There are three strategies I'm going to go over with you that I think will help you learn how to use punctuation effectively in your own writing:

1. Explicit Learning: We all learn punctuation in two ways: *implicitly* (by being exposed to it whenever we read something in English) and *explicitly* (by consciously becoming aware of how it's used and

for what purposes). RLW is a form of explicit learning and the initial strategy upon which the next two are based.

2. Visual Reading: This RLW strategy involves *looking at* the typography of a page or screen that you're reading and *seeing* how punctuation structures the meaning and expression of what we read and write. (If you are nonsighted, of course, this kind of visual reading would be accomplished by setting your screen reader – if possible – to call out all the marks of punctuation on the text being transcribed. I'll tell you when to do that.) When we read with such awareness, we learn explicitly things we already have an implicit familiarity with, including certain rules governing punctuation usage.

3. Aural Reading: This RLW strategy involves *hearing* how the prose in a text flows, often by *listening* to the "tone" of an author's voice. Italics, dashes, exclamation points, and even semicolons help express an author's tone – their attitude toward what they're writing about – as well as illustrate the context of the situation being described. Although this strategy can involve reading aloud and listening to how your own voice is shaped by punctuation, listening *imaginatively* – as some hearing-impaired readers or people who identify themselves as Deaf do – also works wonderfully.

These strategies are not meant to replace standard usage expectations of punctuation described in writing handbooks or online tutorials. They're simply ways to enhance your familiarity with how punctuation operates in written English so that you will use it effectively – *and correctly* – when you write your own texts. You can learn a whole lot about punctuation by becoming explicitly conscious of it while reading. My hope is that by doing so you will begin to think of it less as a set of "rules" and more as a system of conventions with considerable flexibility and important rhetorical effects.

Strategy 1: Learning Explicitly

If you've been writing in formal English for a long time, you probably don't think twice about putting periods at the end of sentences, commas after items in a list, or apostrophes in contractions like "I'm." You just do it out of habit because you've always done it that way (except perhaps when you're texting or messaging with family or friends). Why is that? In some cases, you were taught these standard usage conventions and have remembered them so well that you don't need to think about them anymore. In other cases, your repeated exposure to written English – through story books, novels, textbooks, menus, news articles, signs and posters – has allowed you to learn things without realizing you were learning. Cognitive psychologists and educational researchers call our ability to learn without conscious awareness *implicit learning*. By contrast, they define *explicit learning* as when we are consciously aware of what we're learning, like when we memorize grammar rules or times tables (Ellis, 3). Nancy Mann, a composition and rhetorical theorist, has described punctuation as something that "is often learned without teaching and more often than not learned despite much teaching" (359). She claims that punctuation decisions are often made by writers not because of what they've been explicitly taught in school – the "rules" – but because they have acquired an *unconscious* awareness of its structuring principles simply by reading and writing.

Since day one, we've been learning about the world implicitly as well as explicitly. We don't realize the implicit things we're learning, though, until we become conscious of them. This is how it is with punctuation. Rarely do we become explicitly aware of it unless its' really, not working the, way it should. When punctuation doesn't pop out and announce itself to readers like it does when it's not properly employed, it's invisible.

That's why it's important for us to make it visible. In his *Writing Spaces* essay "How to Read Like a Writer," Mike Bunn describes trying to read books while working in a theater with a lot of noise coming from the stage. By focusing intently on the language as he tried to concentrate, he realized that he was no longer reading like most of us read – as *readers*; instead, he was reading like a *writer*, paying close attention to "the interesting ways authors string words into phrases into paragraphs into entire books" (72). In school, we've been taught to read mainly for information and ideas. When we read for these things we default to reading like *readers*. When we read like *writers*, Bunn tells us, we pay attention to the text, to the choices authors make, the "techniques" they employ, which influence how readers respond to their writing (72). What is this author's main idea? What's their[2] purpose? What facts, descriptions, statistics, and historical accounts do they offer to illustrate or support their purpose or idea? He cites Charles Moran, an English professor at the University of Massachusetts, to illustrate what it means to RLW:

> When we read like writers we understand and participate in the writing. We see the choices the writer has made, and we see how the writer has coped with the consequences of those choices... We "see" what the writer is doing because we read as writers; we see

because we have written ourselves and know the territory, know the feel of it, know some of the moves ourselves. (qtd. in Bunn, 75)

It's interesting that Moran uses the verb *see* several times in this passage – even "quoting" it for emphasis – to illustrate the act of reading like writers. While Moran's seemingly *sensory* approach to reading is more figurative than literal, he's clearly advocating developing habits designed to make us explicitly learn what we already implicitly "know the feel of." Let's literally apply Moran's reading-as-seeing metaphor by explicitly *looking* at the texts we read and *seeing* how punctuation functions in them. I call this next strategy "visual reading."

Strategy 2: Visual Reading

This RLW strategy isn't hard to do, but it can take a little getting used to. Reading visually is something we do all the time. For example, at the beginning of this essay I described a moment in a *Harry Potter* novel when the half-blood wizard Professor Dumbledore explains to young Harry why he calls the villainous Voldermort by his real name and not "the Dark Lord." Even if you have never read a single *Harry Potter* book or seen any of the movie adaptations, when you read my brief description, did you not picture in your mind a smart, wizard-like man giving advice to a young boy about some mean-looking antagonist? If so, then you were in a sense reading visually; the words "wizard," "professor," "young Harry," "villainous," and "Dark Lord" helped paint a picture of a situation involving three different characters. This kind of visual reading, though, is imaginative; we see the situation with our *minds*, not our actual eyes. In order to "see" how punctuation operates in written English, we need to look at it with our eyes. If, however, we are nonsighted or visually impaired (I am actually blind in one eye), then we need to imaginatively "see" the punctuation using a screen reader.

We seldom pay attention to the important ways punctuation shapes our reading of a text because few of us have been encouraged to adopt what composition theorist John Trimbur calls a "typographical perspective." Typography is the appearance and style of printed language. Trimbur points out that essay writing has long been taught as a "process" in which "the page itself is of little account." "As readers," he points out, "we are supposedly not looking at the visual design but following the writer's thoughts" (367). When reading for information, we seldom register what our eyes are actually *seeing*: that "writing is a visible language that is produced and circulated in material forms" (363) like the page you're reading / looking at / seeing right now. When we visually read the typography, we begin to see things that we often take for granted. Punctuation is one of them.

While we may not be accustomed to reading with an explicit awareness of a text's typography, we all do it occasionally. Have you ever had to write a research paper using MLA citation style? If so, you've probably looked at a sample Works Cited page to see how it's set up. You saw, for example, that when citing an article from an academic journal you put the "article's title in quotation marks" and the *journal's title in italics*. You *looked* at the format, *saw* the conventions, and then did the same thing for your own Works Cited page. That's an example of visually reading the typography of a text. With this in mind, I'm now going to ask you to do something kind of strange. You've probably never been asked to do this before, and it may take a moment or two to get used to it. But here goes. When you get to the end of this paragraph, come back and read it again *visually*, from a typographical perspective, so that you "see" the punctuation. With this explicit awareness in mind, think about the purpose or effect of each mark. Are you ready? If so, open your eyes wide (or set your screen reader to call out all the punctuation marks). OK, let's do it. Ready. Get set . . . *Go!*

In the paragraph above, you "saw" ten different marks of punctuation. Some of them I had to use to meet standard usage expectations: periods to end sentences, apostrophes to make contractions or show possession, question marks to indicate questions, and commas to set apart clauses. Other punctuation marks I used – like the em dash, exclamation points, italics, ellipses, quotation marks to create emphasis, and even the parentheses— were optional, *rhetorical choices* I made to emphasize certain things and give my writing a colloquial style. I chose to use an ellipses (. . .) before the italicized exclamation *Go!* in order to create a slight pause and give dramatic effect to the assigned task. I could have used an em dash (Get set – *Go!*) or just a period (Get set. *Go!*), but I know from my own RLW experience that the ellipses is sometimes used to indicate a pause, and I wanted you to get a sense of anticipation, kind of like track runners feel when they're all lined up waiting for the start to a race.

I also know from my own RLW experience that my version of the ellipses is used primarily in informally written texts where readers are supposed to get a sense of the author's personality or attitude toward what they're writing about. Writing informally is another thing I and other *Writing Space* authors do with the hope that you, our student audience, will become engaged by silently listening to our voices as you read. Our writing often "sounds like" we're speaking. And punctuation plays a big role in conveying the tone – be it informal or formal – of an author's voice. Let's turn now to how punctuation can help our writing *sound*.

Strategy 3. Aural Reading

The word *aural* refers to the sense of hearing and, hence, the act of listening. The writing scholar Wendy Bishop tells us that "[i]f all our sentences, all our prose, followed 'the rules' . . . we'd lose something. We'd be bored to death. We wouldn't 'hear' much from texts." She advocates having a "flexible sentence strategy" that is shaped less by our concern with rules than with a desire "to create what we call style—your own best way of saying" (121-22). It's interesting how Bishop describes one's writing style as a way of "saying." A sensory RLW approach involves more than looking at and seeing the elements of a printed text; it involves *listening* to the prose made up of those words as we read. We hear what the writer "says" while reading what they've written.

In addition to contributing to the flow and rhythm of a text, punctuation plays an important role in conveying an author's voice. Voice is a rhetorical convention in multiple genres – blogs, news articles, opinion pieces, business letters, novels, poems, how-to guides, and, of course, essays. When we hear the term *voice* we immediately think of spoken articulation. But writing has voice too, and often that voice has a particular tone. As you read this chapter, can you hear my voice? If so, you'll notice that, like others in *Writing Spaces*, it has an informal tone. I use contractions (*it's, don't*) and personal pronouns (*I, you, we*) in an attempt to convey the impression that I'm talking to you. My purpose is to share with you, my audience, my belief that punctuation matters more than we realize, and part of my rhetorical strategy is to write in a way that personalizes your reading of my essay. If my voice is friendly, conversational, and even a little passionate about *(drumroll, please!)* punctuation, then hopefully you'll keep reading and come to share my view. And as you can see with your own typographically trained eyes, I draw from a battery of punctuation marks to help me out.

I began this chapter with a two-sentence expression that was so poorly punctuated it distracted people from engaging with the meaning. If you go back and read it again, you'll realize that it's almost impossible to read aloud. Because we couldn't really hear what it was saying, it failed to create a context – convey meaning – that we could relate to our own experiences. Let's bring this chapter to a close with another two-sentence expression, but this time I'm going to punctuate the sentences correctly, but in different ways, to demonstrate how punctuation gives a tone of voice to writing. As the punctuation changes, so too does the tone and, along with that, the context of each sentence. When he wrote "How to Read Like A Writer," Mike Bunn asked former students for feedback about how to read effectively in the writing class. One student said it was important to have a "context" for the text you're reading (76). Often that means identifying the author's purpose and intended audience. But context can often be discerned by listening to their tone of voice and identifying their attitude toward the subject or situation being described. As you will see, even though the words remain the same, the punctuation conveys a very different tone and context for a certain situation.

First, let's begin with no punctuation whatsoever. Here is the two-sentence expression:

> they didnt mislead they flat out lied

If the author has an attitude here, it's hard to hear because something essential – punctuation – is missing. It may work as a text message where the writers know the context of what's being discussed, but here it's just messy writing on a page. Let's meet the expectations of readers by putting in some standard punctuation marks. Here's the first version, which I'll call expression **A**:

> They didn't mislead. They flat-out lied.

After capitalizing the first word of each sentence, I put the required apostrophe in the contraction "don't," two periods at the end of both sentences, and a hyphen in the compound adverb "flat-out" (when two words are joined to modify a noun or verb, we connect them with a hyphen). Now that the writing doesn't distract by violating any "rules," I can better hear the writer's voice. It's informal. I can tell by their use of "flat-out" – which is a colloquial, somewhat slangy term meaning *blatantly, purposely, without hesitation* – and their use of the contraction "don't," the informal version of "do not." In addition, the tone of voice provides a little context to the situation being described here. The author seems to be directly stating a fact: They didn't do this. They did that. Period. When I read it aloud and listen to my own voice, it sounds relatively informal but also kind of "factual." There may be a little bias by the author toward the situation here, but the limited punctuation doesn't emphasize it that much.

Now let's listen to how the tone of voice changes when we punctuate this expression differently. First, please visually read the following two expressions from a typographical perspective (or set your screen reader to call out the punctuation marks), seeing how the punctuation marks help to give each one a distinct context. Then, with each context in mind, aurally read it – aloud if possible, or imaginatively with your inner voice – and listen to how your own voice changes to express the differences:

B. They didn't mislead? They flat-out. . . lied?

C. They didn't "mislead." They flat-out *lied*.

The context implied by expression **B** is quite different from expression **A** that we just read. In expression **B,** the writer seems to be surprised by the news that this group of people lied, which is a more egregious act than simply misleading. The ellipses (. . .) gives me the impression that the harsh truth of the matter is slowly dawning on the writer. I therefore aurally read **B** with a naïve and incredulous tone of voice that lilted upwards (which English speakers tend to do when asking questions) and then paused – with a little shudder even – before uttering that fatal final word. The punctuation of expression **C**, on the other hand, gives me the impression that the writer knows precisely what this unethical group of people did. The quotation marks suggest that this group actually used the word "mislead" to diminish the severity of their dishonesty. The author "quotes" their misleading use of "mislead" and then emphasizes that dishonesty by italicizing the word *lied*. Unlike expressions **A** and (especially) **B**, I get the impression of a pretty strong bias here, and so I read aloud **C** with a sarcastic tone of voice, emphasizing the quoted term "mislead" and emphasizing even more strongly the italicized term *lied*.

Do you see how punctuation, by conveying the tone of an author's voice, can also illustrate the context of a situation being described? Although expressions **A**, **B**, and **C** have the same basic structure and describe a specific situation, the punctuation provides us with different ways of perceiving that situation. Interesting, huh? Just don't lose sight of the fact that the punctuation in all three expressions is correctly employed so as not to break any rules and distract readers.

Final Words

As you can see, we can actually learn a lot about writing simply by paying explicit attention to those inconspicuous punctuation marks we're accustomed to gliding over as we read. Sometimes we can even learn the rules themselves, though it's always a good idea to double-check our assumptions with reference to a trustworthy source. Ultimately, though, we should care about punctuation not because of the rules but because of our readers. Writing that's well punctuated is more than just "correct." It's readable, informative, and often even engaging. In short, it's rhetorically effective.

Questions

1. This chapter encourages you to read both visually and aurally so that you *see* and *hear* how punctuation functions in writing. Is this kind of reading something that comes easily to you, or do you have to work at it? Do you think it's possible to read for entertainment or information at the same time that you are paying attention to the look and sound of writing?
2. Some writers who "listen" to writing acknowledge the role punctuation plays in making texts appeal to the ear. Theodor Adorno, a 20th century philosopher, compared punctuation to music (300). The writer Lynn Truss claims that "punctuation directs you how to read, in the way musical notation directs a musician how to play" (20). What do you think about this analogy? What else might you compare punctuation to, and why?
3. In this chapter, the author re-punctuated a two-sentence expression ("They didn't mislead. They flat-out lied.") three ways. A famous philosopher, Rene Descartes, summed up his thinking with a famous axiom "*I think, therefore I am.*" (His original phrase, in Latin, is "*cogito, ergo sum.*") Go online and find out what "*I think, therefore I am*" means philosophically, then think (or talk with your peers) about how the single comma used in the original translation helps to express that idea. Afterwards, re-punctuate this expression in three or four ways so that it has three distinctly different voices and contexts. What would be the "philosophy" of each expression? Have fun with this one.

Notes

1. In "How to Teach Punctuation," Ralph H. Singleton argues that italics is one of several devices that ought to be taught along with punctuation, since their purpose and use are the same (112). In this chapter I treat italics as a form of punctuation.

2. Do you wonder if I made a mistake here? Should I have used "he or she" for "the author," which is singular, instead of "they"? In this instance, I'm using what's called the "singular *they*." The singular *they* is used in common expressions

like "Somebody left their credit card on the restaurant table." Not only is it less cumbersome than "he or she," it's also a gender-neutral term that respectfully includes people who do not identify as either male or female. For these reasons, I use the singular *they* throughout this essay (More here: https://en.wikipedia.org/wiki/Singular_they).

Works Cited

Adorno, Theodor W. "Punctuation Marks." *The Antioch Review*, translated by Shierry Weber Nicholsen, vol. 48, no. 3, 1990, 300-05. *JSTOR*, www.jstor.org/stable/4612221. Accessed 10 May 2019.

Bishop, Wendy. "Reading, Stealing, and Writing Like a Writer." *Elements of Alternate Style: Essays on Writing and Revision*. Ed. Wendy Bishop. Portsmouth, NH: Boynton/Cook, 1997, pp. 119-30

Bunn, Mike. "How to Read Like a Writer." *Writing Spaces, Readings on Writing*, vol. 2, 2010. Eds. Charles Lowe and Pavel Zemliansky. WAC Clearinghouse. Accessed: 10 May 2019. https://writingspaces.org/bunn--how-to-read-like-a-writer

Ellis, Rod. Introduction. "Implicit and Explicit Learning, Knowledge and Instruction." *Implicit and Explicit Knowledge in Second Language Learning, Testing and Teaching*. Ed. Rod Ellis. Multilingual Matters, 2009, pp. 3-26.

Mann, Nancy. "Point Counterpoint: Teaching Punctuation as Information Management." *College Composition and Communication*, vol. 54, no. 3, 2003, pp. 359-93.

Rowling, J. K. *Harry Potter and the Sorcerer's Stone*. Scholastic Press, 1999.

Singleton, Ralph H. "How to Teach Punctuation." *College English*, vol. 6, no. 2, 1944, pp. 111-15.

Trimbur, John. "Delivering the Message: Typography and the Materiality of Writing." *Teaching Composition: Background Readings*. 3rd edition, edited by T. R. Johnson, Bedford St. Martin's, 2007, pp. 363-76.

Truss, Lynne. *Eats, Shoots & Leaves: A Zero Tolerance Approach to Punctuation*. Gotham Books, 2003.

Teacher Resources for Punctuation's Rhetorical Effects by Kevin Cassell

Overview and Teaching Strategies

Punctuation, along with grammar, has long been conceived of in Composition and Writing Studies as a Lower Order Concern. It is not unusual for college and university students to complete two semesters of first year writing without attending to punctuation in any meaningful way. Primarily this oversight – if it can be called that – is a result of the disciplinary privileging of process over product. We all know that knowledge of how to use semicolons and commas effectively is negligible if a writer doesn't have something worth punctuating in the first place. Hence we spend what precious little class time we have with our students focusing on Higher Order Concerns: developing a thesis or claim, writing with a central purpose for a target audience, organizing ideas and information, drafting and revising. We know that punctuation matters – after all, when we ourselves write essays and reports and emails and syllabi, we're generally pretty meticulous about how we use it. But as teachers, we don't have the time to cover the exhaustive number of standard usage expectations, the "rules" governing punctuation, that we've learned over time. That's why so many of us supplement our primary textbooks with writing handbooks (or link to online sites like Purdue Owl), which more often than not are used as a "reference" for students to consult on their own, usually during the editing stage of final drafts.

This essay offers an approach to punctuation that is not based on "rules." It doesn't tell students how to use punctuation correctly. Instead, it encourages them to become explicitly aware of punctuation as they read by *seeing* and *hearing* it, and ultimately *understanding* how it's employed for what purposes. Standard usage expectations or "rules" are just one way of learning punctuation; reading with an awareness of how those marks (, : " ? ; **b** ' *i* –) operate in standard written English across multiple genres is a significant first step to learning punctuation – and many of us, I think, have learned usage in this manner. Yes, we need to know certain usage rules, but these can often be discerned (and sometimes implicitly learned) from reading with an awareness of punctuation as a textual feature that shapes phrases, sentences, and paragraphs. Writing handbooks, online tutorials and guides are not the only way for students to become familiar with punctuation usage.

I introduce punctuation in my FYW courses early in the semester. I don't discuss it solely in terms of editing and proofreading final drafts for the sake of correctness. Instead, I point out that it is a material and rhetorical element in the texts they read and plays a role in their reception of those texts. As shown in my essay, I distinguish between punctuation usage that is "required" (apostrophes to show contractions or possession, question marks for questions, periods to end sentences) and usage that is more flexible and oftentimes rhetorical (parentheses or em dashes, italics or bold, ellipses). I introduce students to the strategy of explicit reading, which I associate in my chapter, following Charles Moran and Mike Bunn, with "reading like a writer" (RLW). I bring up punctuation throughout the course, when appropriate, and often in relation to Higher Order Concerns like purpose, context, and especially audience. For example, when reading an essay – like a *Writing Spaces* chapter – I'll ask students to choose a particular paragraph where the author makes a salient point or just says something memorable. After discussing that point in relation to the essay's purpose, I'll ask them to consider *how* that point or memorable statement is conveyed. This leads inevitably to the text of that paragraph and the sentences, words, and – yes – punctuation marks that compose it. Sometimes that punctuation supports an "aural" representation of an author's voice (like my use of two em dashes around the word "yes" in the previous sentence), which provides an occasion to consider how audience awareness informs certain choices the author makes during the writing process that are sometimes supported punctuationally.

I have emphasized multimodal reading strategies – reading as "seeing" and "hearing" especially – for some years now. (I don't use the term multimodal in my chapter; I use the more common term "sensory.") I believe that this style of reading, because it makes students conscious of how language functions as writing, helps them develop as writers. While I don't eschew "rules," "guidelines," and "best practices," I believe that one of the best ways to learn how to write is to read with an awareness of writing – to read like a writer. With the exception of some text messages perhaps, punctuation is something we encounter every time we read across all genres. Because we tend to read for information and ideas, however, punctuation tends to slip out of sight. The 20th century thinker Theodor Adorno called punctuation "inconspicuous." What I try to do is have it visually and aurally register with the eyes and ears of readers so that it is less inconspicuous. I believe that being mindful of, first, the material existence of punctuation in writing, and second, of its effective employment will help students use it with confidence and facility in their own writing.

Activities

1. Have students choose one punctuation mark that they feel they don't know as well as they'd like to. Have students go online or look in their writing handbook at how this mark is used, then share that usage skill with others.
2. Have students pair up. Working separately, ask them to find a short paragraph from an essay, article, or book that has a variety of punctuation marks in it. Have them write that paragraph down on a piece of paper, taking out all of the punctuation marks. Student pairs should exchange paragraphs and be instructed to punctuate their partner's paragraph. Ask students to compare the original with their punctuated paragraph, seeing how close both students came to the original, and have students discuss why they chose some of the marks they did.

2 Understanding Visual Rhetoric

Jenae Cohn

Overview

Visuals can dramatically impact our understanding of a rhetorical situation. In a writing class, students do not always think that they will need to be attentive to visuals, but visual information can be a critical component to understanding and analyzing the rhetorical impacts of a multimodal text. This chapter gives examples of what visual rhetoric looks like in everyday situations, unpacking how seemingly mundane images like a food picture on social media or a menu at a restaurant, can have a persuasive impact on the viewer. The chapter then offers students some terms to use when describing visuals in a variety of situations.

Introduction

It's Friday night and you're hungry.* So, you corral some friends and you all decide that you'd like to go out to eat somewhere new. You hop online to explore your options, and, in the process, you find a wealth of information from menus and visitor reviews to hours and locations. But there's one factor that has an especially strong influence on your choice: the pictures of the food.

---

* This work is licensed under the Creative Commons Attribution-NonCommercial-NoDerivatives 4.0 International License (CC BY-NC-ND 4.0) and are subject to the Writing Spaces Terms of Use. To view a copy of this license, visit http://creativecommons.org/licenses/by-nc-nd/4.0/, email info@creativecommons.org, or send a letter to Creative Commons, PO Box 1866, Mountain View, CA 94042, USA. To view the Writing Spaces Terms of Use, visit http://writingspaces.org/terms-of-use.

Understanding Visual Rhetoric   19

Figure 1. A cheeseburger is held in a close-up shot. Photo by Jenae Cohn.

Figure 2. A hamburger and fries meal at Shake Shack in Palo Alto, California. Photo by Jenae Cohn.

You check out a review page for a hamburger joint and find yourself drooling over a close-up shot of a juicy burger with a slice of cheese oozing over the edge (see figure 1). You click to the next shot and see a cascade of golden french fries on a tray with an ombre-tinted iced tea and lemonade (see figure 2). You click one more time and find yet another delectable shot: a frosty milkshake with a mountain of whipped cream on top. You're feeling increasingly convinced that this restaurant is where you'll suggest that you and your friends go out to eat.

You decide to click through to see one more picture, expecting to see yet another culinary delight (see figure 3). But this next photo surprises you: it's a picture of someone's tray of food, but it's dimly lit and a little hard to tell what's there. The hamburger looks squished and flat, the meat greasy and paltry. The french fries curled up next to the burger look a bit dried out. There's a mysterious puddle of sauce in a bowl next to the plate burger, and it's not totally clear what's in it. The meal suddenly doesn't look so appetizing after all.

Figure 3. A poorly lit, squished hamburger and fries. Photo by Jenae Cohn.

You find yourself confused. All of these pictures are supposedly of food at the same restaurant, but the pictures look so different from each other. Knowing that the images may not accurately reflect the reality of the restaurant experience, you feel angry and misled: how can you possibly know which photos capture the "real" experience at the restaurant? Why trust any photos of restaurant food at all?

The fact of the matter is that you can't know *exactly* what your restauranting experience will be like when you walk in the door of a new place. But the images clearly had a persuasive impact on you as a decision-maker: the contrast between the appetizing images and the unappetizing photos made you question the quality and consistency of the restaurant's food, a contrast that made you wonder whether the restaurant would be the kind of place where you'd like to visit.

The point here is those photos of the food you found at the restaurant impacted your decision-making, which makes them a perfect example of visual rhetoric in action. Visual rhetoric refers to any communicative moment where visuals (photographs, illustrations, cartoons, maps, diagrams, etc.) contribute to making meaning and displaying information. You're in a writing class right now (which is probably why you're reading this essay and wondering what hamburgers have to do with anything), and you may think of writing mostly as words on the page. However, as more writers publish and distribute their work online, the more readers expect to find that information may be communicated in multiple modes, from text to visuals and audio. As writing and rhetoric scholar Carolyn Handa puts it,

> rhetoric's association with the written word is arbitrary, a by-product of print culture rather than the epistemological limits of rhetoric itself. We use rhetoric to help us think more clearly, write more elegantly, design more logically. Rhetoric works both to scaffold our ideas for clearer understanding and to structure our critical examinations of both visual and verbal objects. (2)

What Handa means by "the epistemological limits of rhetoric itself" (and yes, that is a mouthful!) is that, when we think of making meaning, building arguments, and reaching our target audiences, we are not limited to words as a tool. In fact, if we limit ourselves to words in our arguments, we may not successfully reach our audiences at all. Some audiences need visuals to think through an idea, and using graphs and diagrams can express some ideas *more* clearly than text can. So, we have to take visuals into account as part of understanding communication.

You may be thinking that this all sounds good, but what about images that are just pretty for the sake of being pretty? Well, those exist too, but we call those "art." A picture of a hamburger framed in an art museum does not exist to market hamburgers (though it might make you hungry!). However, a picture of a hamburger on an Instagram feed for a particular restaurant exists as a way to encourage visitors to come and dine at the restaurant. As composition scholar and teacher Kristen Welch describes it: "visual rhetoric is a focus on the practical, relevant, and functional as opposed to an aesthetic analysis or use of visual elements for beauty" (256). It is important to recognize when a visual exists to help us appreciate beauty (and we may even appreciate the beauty of a picture of a hamburger on an Instagram feed), but the context in which we see visuals matters an awful lot in terms of how we analyze and understand their impacts on us as viewers.

Our example of finding food photos from a restaurant online exemplifies just how accessible visual rhetoric really is in our everyday lives. Clearly, the lighting, composition, and angle of the image clearly makes a big difference in our reaction to the image and potentially our willingness to take action and respond to the image (either by going to the restaurant or not). After reading through the opening story, you may have thought of lots of other ways that you encounter other pictures of food online. On social media, for example, a lot of users post images of food they've cooked or eaten as a way to share eating experiences. Because of how consumer interests are driven by the platforms they use to access information, visuals are more important than ever for people to make decisions or become attracted to visiting particular spaces. But visual rhetoric is not just about persuading someone to like something or not. Visual rhetoric can also be used to help people understand a concept, break down an idea, or access important pieces of information.

We'll explore a few more examples of what visual rhetoric can look like in a few other situations where the visuals may not just be persuasive, but they may offer necessary guidance or instruction for the viewer. After that, this chapter will offer you some advice on how you might analyze visuals in your future writing classes so that you, too, can interpret the visuals you encounter in rhetorical situations.

Why Do Visuals Matter?

Let's think back to the restaurant example one more time. You've picked a restaurant for your Friday night dinner and now you're with your friends and are seated at the dining table. A waiter hands you a menu and guess what? You're seeing yet another example of visual rhetoric in action. This particular menu comes from a real restaurant, called Oren's Hummus, which has locations around the San Francisco Bay Area in California (see figure 4).

Figure 4. An image of a menu for Oren's Hummus with three columns containing various menu items. Menu image courtesy of Mistie Cohen.

This restaurant menu doesn't have pictures on it, but it makes visual choices that may impact which food items you decide to order. For example, separating certain food items under headers, like "Hummus Bowls" and "Grilled Entrees" gives you some quick visual information about what items you can expect to find in those sections. Even more noticeably, the section titled "Dips & Sides" is separated from the other menu items by a green box. While the words "Dips & Sides" may have helped us understand that the items in that section would be smaller-sized than the menu items outside the green box, the use of the green box is a rhetorical tool; it makes it really obvious to the restaurant goer that if they order an item from the Dips & Sides section, it's going to be smaller than the items that are not inside the green box.

Think about this particular restaurant's context even more: the restaurant advertises its "hummus," a Mediterranean dip made out of garbanzo beans, in its name, but for many visitors, they may not have experienced eating hummus in the way that this restaurant serves it. For many diners, they may have experienced hummus as a dip or side rather than as a main course. However, because "Hummus Bowls" appear on the menu separately from the Dips & Sides, it's clear that the hummus bowls can actually be eaten as a main dish rather than as a side dish. This is a new situation, a subversion of expectations, for many restaurant-goers, so the menu has to do some visual work to help the visitor understand what to expect from the food they order.

Do you see how many words it took me to explain how the Dips & Sides section differs from the other menu sections? If you were a hungry diner, would you want to take the time to listen to all of that or read that long explanation? Probably not. That's why the document design on the menu is so important: it aligns our expectations quickly, simply, and clearly. Document design is yet another example of visual rhetoric in action, as it persuades us to make particular choices (in this case, about what we order). To learn more about components of document design in particular, you may want to look to another essay in the *Writing Spaces* series, called "Beyond Black on White: Document Design and Formatting in the Writing Classroom" by Michael J. Klein and Kristi L. Shackleford. They make the important case that, "Good document design integrates the words on the page with appropriate imagery to fully illustrate your meaning," a sentiment that reflects exactly what we saw happen with the menu (333).

The menu also includes some symbols to indicate which menu items may adhere to particular dietary needs, a piece of visual information that may be critical to those with allergies or sensitivities. Next to the descriptions of particular menu items, the letters "gf" and "v" indicate which items on the menu are "gluten free" (items that don't contain binding proteins found in wheat and other grains) or "vegan" (items that don't contain animal products, like meat or dairy); a key for these restrictions is in the bottom right-hand corner of the menu for visitors to reference if they are seeking out those indications.

Some menus will indicate these dietary restrictions using visual symbols instead; for example, other menus may include a green leaf icon next to particular items to indicate that the menu item is vegetarian or a brown-colored "G" inside a circle often indicates that the menu item is gluten-free. While you, as a reader, may have some critiques of how clearly the Oren's Hummus menu makes these dietary restrictions clear, the point is that the visual indicators are there to guide visitors in critical ways.

You may also notice that, on the menu, the two biggest visual items are the restaurant's logo and slogan ("Rip, Scoop, Eat!") and the inclusion of "Gluten Free Pita" on its menu. These largest items show the restaurant's priorities: by making its slogan and name large, the menu reminds you of its branding, while also offering you an instruction for enjoying its signature dishes: to rip a piece of pita, scoop the pita into dip, and eat it! Making the words "Gluten Free Pita" among the largest on the menu also suggests that the restaurant aims to reach a diversity of diners, even those who may be sensitive to or avoiding eating wheat-based products. The restaurant's priorities are clear: to educate unfamiliar hummus-eaters with the process and experience of eating hummus while also convincing diners that, regardless of their dietary restrictions, there will likely be something at the restaurant that the diner will enjoy.

The point of all this analysis of the Oren's Hummus menu is that choices in document text, color, image, and spacing matter in order to help you make choices, big and small. As you can see, visuals play a tremendous role in a) how we make decisions, b) how we receive instructions, and c) how we understand information. But let's get a little bit more fine-grained: what elements of visual design exactly can help make certain ideas clearer than others? How do we name and define the persuasive elements of a visual? Let's look to some elements of visual design to answer those questions.

ELEMENTS OF VISUAL DESIGN: LINE, COLOR, SHAPE, SIZE, SPACE, VALUE, TEXTURE

The elements of visual design are one way to help us understand more clearly why a visual has a particular kind of effect on its viewer. The elements of visual design may not necessarily help us understand purpose or intent, but they can help us break down different component parts of images so that we can start to puzzle out what an image might do for us as viewers and readers. We, naturally, should understand these elements in their particular contexts, and the impacts of these elements will likely differ depending on where and how we're viewing a particular image. With that said, beginning to name what we notice is one important step to gathering more information about images so that we can articulate their meaning more clearly.

Here are six elements of visual design you may want to consider in order to understand how an image is communicating a particular idea.

Line

Lines are visual markers that are often used to divide different sections of an image or document into multiple parts. Lines can create order in something disorderly, offering the eyes a sense of where to go or how to differentiate between different elements. Many artists and graphic designers often rely on grids of lines to help them determine where to place particular elements in a picture or a graphic to ensure that the viewer can understand where to focus their attention or where to differentiate one piece of information from another (see figure 5).

Figure 5. The edge of an orange fence casts a shadow on the sidewalk. Image is titled "lines" by Charlotte Kinzie (www.flickr.com/photos/ckinzie/252835206) and is licensed under CC BY-NC-ND 2.0

When you look at a visual, consider asking questions about line in the following ways:

- What role is the line playing in helping me understand what to emphasize? What to deemphasize?
- What role is the line playing in connecting one part of the image with the other? What relationships between the parts of the image are at play?
- What kind of pattern do I see in this image or diagram? How does the pattern help shape my understanding of the image, graph, or shape?

Color

Color can help evoke emotions in the viewer while also helping the viewer distinguish what's important or what should be emphasized. In fact, many designers use resources like color wheels to help them determine what kinds of color combinations complement each other and what kinds of color combinations offer contrast (see figure 6). It is generally agreed upon that particular colors evoke different emotions than others; for example, colors like orange and red tend to convey warmth or passion while colors like blue and purple tend to convey coolness or calm.

However, some colors have deep cultural associations. For example, in China, the color red tends to signify good luck, joy, and happiness; that's why gifts given at Chinese New Year's tend to be in red envelopes and also why wedding dresses in China are often red-colored. In Western cultures, on the other hand, red can more often signify danger or caution. In the United States, we may think of red as the color for a stop sign, for example.

Lots of resources online exist to help designers keep particular cultural associations with color in mind, especially in sensitive situations! For example, while wearing black to a funeral in the United States would be conventional and respectful, it would actually be considered quite odd to wear black to a funeral in Cambodia, where the color white is much more often worn for events of mourning.

You may not be able to account for all of the different situations where colors may signify different things to different viewers, but as a reader and composer, you will want to be attentive to how and where color is used, even if the possibilities for interpretation may vary.

Figure 6. An abstract pattern of rectangles in a variety of muted earth tones, ranging from oranges to greens, blues, and browns. Image is titled "color swatches" by Nancy Muller (www.flickr.com/photos/kissabug/2469838932) and is licensed under CC BY-NC-ND 2.0.

When you look at a visual, consider asking questions about color in the following ways:

- What is color (or the lack of color if the visual is black-and-white) emphasizing here? What is de-emphasized?
- Given my understanding of color, what emotions does the color evoke for me? What do the colors in the image remind me of?
- How might this visual change if the color scheme was inverted? How would the impact on the viewer be altered?

Shape

All visuals contain elements that take on different *shapes* (see figure 7). We probably learned about shapes at some point when we were children, especially if we played with toy blocks. Have you ever seen toy blocks in the shapes of squares, triangles, and circles? If so, congratulations, you've had exposure to the three basic shape types that exist in the world!

Many other shapes build off of these three fundamental shape types. For example, in the natural world, we may easily recognize shapes like clouds, trees, and water droplets. Similarly, certain man-made objects take on particular meanings through their shapes alone. For example, lightbulbs are shapes that typically symbolize new or "bright" ideas, while the shape of a rocket or airplane often signifies innovation or the accomplishment of a goal.

Shapes that come from the real world—like the clouds and trees or the light bulbs and rocket ships—tend to be culturally situated in the same way that colors can have different cultural associations. Yet as readers of visuals, we can analyze the roles that shapes play based on our own understanding of the audience's needs and purposes when accessing the visual.

Figure 7. A pattern of circles, squares, and triangles in bright colors contrasted on an asphalt surface. Image is titled "DSC_1384" by Michael Poitrenaud (www.flickr.com/photos/michel_poitrenaud/10595502904) and is licensed under CC BY-NC-SA 2.0.

When you look at a visual, consider asking questions about shapes in the following ways:

- What does this shape typically signify? Where have I seen this kind of shape before?

- Given my understanding of this shape, what emotions does the shape evoke for me?
- What might the shape be drawing attention to?

Size

In visuals, different elements may be large while other elements may be small. Typically, the elements that are larger sizes than other elements are of greater importance than the elements that are smaller sizes. But larger things are not always more valuable; the other elements in the visual may visually draw attention to smaller-sized items so that we don't lose sight of the smaller parts of the visual entirely. Large images next to small images may also be used to help us compare two parts so that we can see how they are related to each other (see figure 8).

Figure 8. A row of three giraffes, ranging from a small giraffe to a larger one, line up outside of a doorway. Image is titled "Giraffes" by Smallbrainfield (www.flickr.com/photos/smallbrainfield/3378461407) and is licensed under CC BY-NC 2.0.

When you look at a visual, consider asking questions about size in the following ways:

- Which elements in the visual are larger than the other elements?

- How do the sizes of different elements in the visual impact your understanding of what's in the visual?
- What is your reaction to seeing the different sizes in the visual? Do any of the sizes of the elements surprise you? Why or why not?

Space

In between or around the elements in a particular visual, there is always some empty space. Some designers call this "white space" or "neutral space." Space is critical to help distinguish between the different elements in a visual. Without space, particular elements in the visual may be hard to distinguish or may have the effect that the visual is "busy" and, therefore, hard to read and understand.

Even in a document that is mostly text, space signifies meaning. For example, when you split paragraphs into their individual units, the space before and after the paragraph indicates that one thought is about to begin while another thought ends. Similarly, in other kinds of visuals, space might help a certain element stand out from other parts or it might help you understand where one part of the image begins and another part ends (see figure 9).

Figure 9. Two red apples are clustered in one corner of a wooden table, drawing attention to the fruit in an open space. Image is titled "apples" by Paul Bausch (*www.flickr.com/photos/pb/6129499766/*) and is licensed under CC BY-NC-SA 2.0.

When you look at a visual, consider asking questions about space in the following ways:

- How much "white space" or "neutral space" is there in the visual? Is this space evenly distributed or are the spaces uneven?
- What effect does the space in this visual have? How does the space break up or distinguish different elements of the visual?
- What is your reaction to seeing the space in the visual?

VALUE

Value refers to the lightness or darkness of a particular element in a visual. For example, think of a visual that may use different shades of the color blue; the elements that are darker blue than the lighter blue elements convey that the darker blue elements have greater *value* than the lighter blue elements. Just as something that is larger in size may signify greater importance than something that is smaller in size, something that is darker in color tends to signify greater value than something that is lighter in color.

Value is a comparative function by default; a dark color by itself may not mean anything unless a lighter color is present by comparison. Similarly, a "dark" visual may not necessarily have greater value than a "light" visual; however, if there are both dark and light elements in a particular visual, those shades signify differing levels of importance or attention in the visual itself. Sometimes, the dark elements may be meant to obscure information and make the lighter elements more visible. At other times, darker shades of a particular color may draw more attention to them than lighter shades of a color (see figure 10).

Figure 10. Light illuminates a dirt pathway in a forest; the trees around the pathway are shaded. Image is titled "West Highland Way" by tomsflickrfotos2 (flickr.com/photos/tomsflickrfotos2/453754005/) and is licensed under CC BY-NC-SA 2.0.

When you look at a visual, consider asking questions about value in the following ways:

- How do different values create importance? Depth? What is emphasized?
- What effect does value in this visual have? How does value break up or distinguish different elements of the visual?
- What is your reaction to seeing different values of visual depth in this visual?

Texture

We may think of texture primarily from a tactile perspective initially. When we touch different objects, we tend to notice texture right away: silk tend to be smooth to the touch while burlap tends to be rough and bumpy. But we can look at a picture and detect different surfaces just by the look of it too, and the conveyance of those textures may also impact our orientation and understanding of what the image conveys. For example, a visual that includes lots of tiny dots may convey a bumpy texture while a visual that includes lots of wavy lines and wavy images may convey a smoother or more "watery" texture. Textures might be used to evoke particular sensations in the viewer, but they may also be used to distinguish one visual element from another (see figure 11).

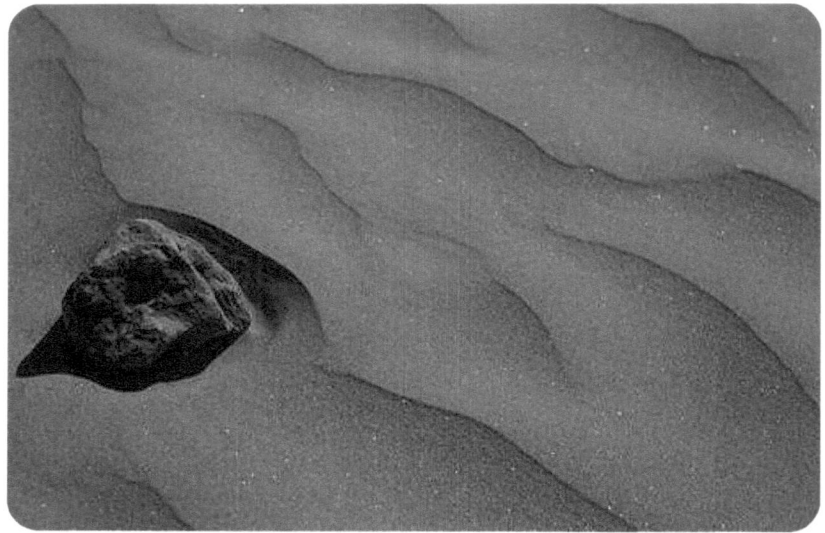

Figure 11. A craggy-textured rock is on the rippled sandy shore of a beach. Image is titled "Beach on the Chang Jiang (Yangtze)" by Eul Mulot (https://www.flickr.com/photos/mulot/3315444069) and is licensed under CC BY-NC-SA 2.0.

When you look at a visual, consider asking questions about texture in the following ways:

- What kinds of textures do I see in this visual? Are textures clearly implied or does the visual just include one kind of texture?
- What effect does texture (or the lack of texture) have on understanding what I should focus on in this image? How does texture break up or distinguish different elements of the visual?
- What is your reaction to seeing different textures in this visual?

Concluding Thoughts

Once we start noticing the role that visuals play all around us, we gain a greater awareness of the range of strategies that communicators use to get our attention. This chapter is just a start in helping you to recognize some examples of visual rhetoric and the roles that visuals can play to help make meaning and persuade others. There is a lot more to learn about designing and making your own visuals. But just as reading will help you become a better writer, viewing and training your eye to recognize what's happening in images will help you to become a better designer.

As you look ahead to thinking capaciously about the strategies you might use to employ images and other media in your writing, bear in mind that not all of your readers will have equal access to all of the communicative strategies you're employing. For visuals in particular, you may have readers who are visually impaired or blind and may not be able to understand or recognize the role that your images are playing in your text. However, as a writer, there are some strategies you can use to help your reader appreciate your use of visuals even if they are not able to see images in the same way that you can. Captions (as you saw included in this chapter) and alternative text (for Web-based images) are ways that you, as a writer, can describe what's happening in a picture so that even if a reader cannot see the image, they can get a sense of what the picture might look like and what effect the picture is having on the document itself.

A picture is often worth a thousand words because it implies so much and can give us a lot of information quickly. Seeing may not always be believing, but visual rhetoric can be a pretty powerful way to help people understand an idea differently than they may have otherwise.

Works Cited

Handa, Carolyn. *Visual Rhetoric in a Digital World: A Critical Sourcebook*. Bedford/St. Martins, 2004.

Klein, Michael J., and Kristi L. Shackelford. "Beyond Black on White: Document Design and Formatting in the Writing Classroom." *Writing Spaces: Readings on Writing*, edited by Charles Lowe and Pavel Zemliansky, vol II, Parlor Press, 201, pp. 333-349. http://writingspaces.org/klein-schackleford--beyond-black-on-white.

Welch, Kristen, Nicholas Lee, and Dustin Shuman. "Teaching Visual Rhetoric in the First-Year Composition Classroom." *Teaching English in the Two-Year College* vol. 37, no. 3 March 2010, pp. 256-264.

Teacher Resources for Understanding Visual Rhetoric by Jenae Cohn

Overview and Teaching Strategies

This essay is intended as an overview of what visual rhetoric is and how it functions alongside other rhetorical strategies that students may encounter in their composition courses. This essay could work well in a unit introducing students to definitions of "rhetoric" so that students can continue to complicate their understanding of rhetoric beyond alphabetic text. This chapter may also be useful to introduce a unit on multimodal composition, especially when students are starting to look at examples of model multimodal texts and understanding the role that visuals may play in those texts. Students may have varying degrees of abilities to describe or name the effects that visuals may have on an audience, and this reading is intended to help students articulate the rhetorical work that visuals do while also giving them some vocabulary to name the basic elements of a visual. This chapter focuses primarily on the analysis of visuals rather than on the composition of visuals, so bear in mind that this chapter does not include tool suggestions or any "how-to" tips on creating visuals. This chapter also does not cover best practices on attributing images appropriately (via Creative Commons licensing, for example) though a conversation around visual rhetoric for multimodal composing should orient students to these best practices so that students understand how to use and incorporate images legally and ethically into their work.

In this chapter, I bring in examples that are accessible to a diverse student populace. That said, it may be worth engaging in class conversation about the ways in which certain visuals may have different effects on different audiences, as particular pieces of iconography or certain photographs may be understood differently by audiences with various cultural backgrounds or experiences. When selecting images for students to choose or analyze, bringing in historical or cultural context is useful since that information may shape students' abilities to understand the rhetorical purpose and situation for particular visuals.

Here I offer several in-class activities that I regularly use in line with the conversations offered in the textbook chapter to supplement what the chapter introduces.

QUESTIONS

1. In the first section of this essay, you experienced the story of choosing a restaurant to dine out at with your friends. In this story, the different kinds of pictures shaped the decision made. When have you made a decision based on pictures or visuals? How did the pictures or visuals affect your decision exactly?
2. In the discussion of the menu from Oren's Hummus, it's clear that the organization and design of the information may impact how a diner might decide what to eat. If you had the opportunity to re-design the menu at Oren's, what decisions would you make? Why would you make those decisions?
3. There are six elements of visual design named in this chapter. Which of these elements were new to you? Which were ones you had encountered before? Individually or in a small group, take a look at either a picture of a poster from the Works Progress Administration (www.loc.gov/pictures/collection/wpapos/) OR find a photograph from the Associated Press images database (www.apimages.com/) and see if you and your group members can identify the elements of design in one or two of the historical posters or photographs. Use the guiding questions in the "Elements of Visual Design" section of the chapter to help guide your understanding of the images.

ACTIVITIES

The following are four class activities that can help support students in their development of understanding and interpreting visual rhetoric.

THREE KEYWORDS.

Pick an image, photograph, or data visualization for the whole class to look at together. You may want to pick something that is related to a topic that the class has been discussing or perhaps something that could act as a source for an upcoming research assignment that the students will conduct. Project or share the visual in a shared space and ask each student to come up with three keywords that they would use to describe the image. Students may submit their three keywords to a polling platform (like PollEverywhere, Google Forms, or a quiz feature in a learning management system) so that all of the results are anonymized and collected in one place. When every student has submitted their three keywords, display or share the results to the class. Use the keywords as conversation points to discuss the different impacts the visuals had on different users. How did the keywords overlap? Where did they differ? How might the keywords that students identified align with how they might analyze and contextualize the impact of the visual? Another discussion point may be to consider how their keywords might have changed if they encountered the visual in a different context or situation.

Extreme Makeover: Document Edition

Ask each student to identify an essay, multimodal project, or class assignment. It can be something that they produced for your class or for a different class. After they've picked the project they've made, ask them to analyze the design choices for the document. What size fonts did they choose? What kinds of pictures did they include, if any? What were some other choices in terms of the document and visual design that they made? Ask them to name the audience and purpose for the document too so that they recognize and name the full context for creating the document. Then, ask them to consider who else might have had a stake in the document they produced. Is there a different audience that they can imagine being invested in that piece of work? Once the students have each named an alternative or a secondary audience for the document, ask them to take a few minutes to do an extreme "makeover" on the document, considering how they would change the layout, organization, design, and inclusion of visuals to accommodate the new audience's needs. An alternative for them would be to consider how they would redesign the document for publication in a particular platform or news site aggregate, like Buzzfeed or The Huffington Post. These platforms might also change the way they're orienting the text as well, but for the purposes of this exercise, you may want to encourage students to think primarily about the visuals. After they've done a version of their "extreme makeover," engage in a conversation about the makeover process. What elements of the design did they decide to change? How did their understanding of audience and purpose impact their visual choices?

Comparing Data Visualizations

Pick a few data visualizations (i.e. infographics) from sites like Information is Beautiful (https://informationisbeautiful.net/) or FlowingData (https://flowingdata.com/) (both of which have large databases of data visualizations and infographics available). Put students into small groups and ask them to analyze what they notice in the data visualizations. What kind of information is being communicated? What is the purpose of using the infographic? How would the understanding of the information differ if it was displayed in text rather than in visuals? How does seeing the visual alter their understanding of the content? A follow-up activity may be to invite them to visualize an aspect of their own writing projects (or research projects) using one of the techniques in the example data visualizations that they explored.

CAPTION CONTEST: CREATING EFFECTIVE CAPTIONS AND ALT-TEXT FOR IMAGE

Asking students to write captions for images can be a really interesting moment for students to interrogate and unpack their assumptions about particular images and what they're privileging as viewers and authors of multimodal or image-rich projects. A conversation about captions can also be a good opportunity to help students understand accessibility and ways to make images readable for a variety of audiences. To start this class activity, you will want to define two different kinds of image captions that exist for visuals published on the Web: captions and alt text. The caption is the text that displays below an image (much like what you would see in a printed textbook and in this particular textbook chapter for that matter). Alt text, on the other hand, is a short, written description of an image Web authors use to describe an image in a sentence for someone using screen reader software. For a reader using screen reader software, the alt text and the caption are both read to offer clarity on what the visual includes. For this class activity, project an image or photograph in a shared space and ask everyone in the class to write both a caption and alt text for the image. You may find it useful to show a few examples of captions and alt text to help clarify the activity. Alternatively, you could have students start with writing captions (since students may have more exposure to reading captions than alt text) and then move to alt text. After students have written their captions, ask them to share with a partner, comparing how their captions are similar or different. Each pair should then take a few minutes to decide which caption they would use for the photo or image if they were publishing the image themselves, justifying their choice as a pair. The results can then be shared with the class where the instructor can lead a longer class conversation about the impacts of captions and the challenges in writing captions to capture the impacts of visuals on the audience.

3 How to Write Meaningful Peer Response Praise

Ron DePeter

Overview

Praise is an important element of peer and teacher feedback—it can, to quote Donald Daiker, "lift the hearts, as well as the pens" of student authors—but substantive praise is one of the most challenging modes of feedback to compose (112). How can writing instructors move student responders beyond standard comments such as "Great paper!" or "I liked it" or "Good details"? This chapter is a guide for students in composition classes, and aims to help them understand the importance of giving and receiving detailed, conversational praise; it presents scenarios for conceptualizing how to write praise, provides sample student writing excerpts that invite students to practice writing praise, offers and analyzes examples of different types of student-authored praise comments, and provides an array of approaches to writing praise comments.

In some first year writing classes, peer feedback days parallel the characters' journey into the Appalachian caves in Neil Marshall's horror film *The Descent*.* A group of female friends goes on an annual thrill-seeking adventure, climbing their way through a complex, uncharted cave, only to encounter some ferocious monsters, as well as their own inner demons. Vivian Sobchack characterizes the chaos depicted in the film this way: "Eventually trapped within the cave system by a rock slide, the six women become separated, each person or little group fitfully lit through different means to allow us to see their struggles in stroboscopic glimpses—and then often to wish we hadn't" (41).

---

* This work is licensed under the Creative Commons Attribution-NonCommercial-NoDerivatives 4.0 International License (CC BY-NC-ND 4.0) and are subject to the Writing Spaces Terms of Use. To view a copy of this license, visit http://creativecommons.org/licenses/by-nc-nd/4.0/, email info@creativecommons.org, or send a letter to Creative Commons, PO Box 1866, Mountain View, CA 94042, USA. To view the Writing Spaces Terms of Use, visit http://writingspaces.org/terms-of-use.

Comparing the film to a first year writing class, the "descent" into peer feedback can sometimes leave all parties lost and helpless: we teachers bemoan the ragged and inconsistent quality of some peer comments, and you, who often complain *only* to us when your peers do a slack job writing comments on your work. Too often, all of us "wish we hadn't" wasted time at all doing peer response.

A few years ago, I had a student (we'll call him Ray) whose peer response routine involved shuffling through his peers' papers—which were to be responded to as homework—and writing generic comments quickly at the start of class. "Good opening," he would write, then next to each paragraph, "Give examples," and at the bottom, "I like the ending, but maybe expand." I began to realize all his comments were the same, and a student who was in his group confirmed that he never read his partners' essays before writing feedback.

Now, that's a *descent*.

Why go into the cave at all, we might ask, especially if even one of your peers approaches the task with such disregard? Or, what about the fact that some writers ignore your feedback anyway, preferring to only pay attention to the instructor's comments, because "they are the one giving the grade"?

Not too long ago, Fred, a student taking his second composition course with me, told his group as he handed his peer feedback to them: "You can ignore these; I'm just trying to get plusses on my feedback." (I assign grades of Plus, Check, or Check Minus on feedback, with some brief commentary about how responders could improve next time.) I was struck by Fred's admission, and his willingness to participate in writing peer responses that he didn't fully stand behind.

The psychology going on in peer groups reminds me of some of the conclusions I drew working on my dissertation on peer response while a graduate student at Florida State University. I collected and studied my students' peer feedback and their thoughts about the feedback they gave/received. I noticed that:

- Students placed greater value in professors' feedback vs. peers', usually ignoring peer responses unless they were forced to use them in revisions;
- Students often felt poorly qualified to write meaningful responses, since they saw themselves as merely adequate, "not good enough to tell someone else how to write;"

- Students were often reluctant to write questions, which they viewed as critical, because they did not want to be perceived as "judging" their peers' experiences, thoughts, or feelings;
- Students would often judge their peers' writing based on what they thought a teacher would want, rather than their own criteria for what makes writing good; and
- Students initially tended to comment on things that were easier to "fix" like grammar or spelling mistakes, and paragraph size.

You may see yourself in one or more of these attitudes, and you may have received or given feedback similarly to Ray or Fred. Such attitudes and approaches are natural: given how sensitive the act of sharing an essay can be, these attitudes and others create a complex dynamic in small groups, leading some of us to prefer to avoid peer feedback, especially if we have not established trust with our group. As a result of these ways of thinking, some writers become frustrated working in small groups, because they don't put much faith in the process or in the weak comments they anticipate receiving.

As a way of free falling right into this metaphorical dark cave, let's jumpstart your class discussion of peer response strategies. I recognize that there are additional types of feedback, such as asking questions, giving advice, and editing or correcting errors, but this essay is going to focus on one important type of feedback.

How to Write Meaningful Praise

Think of a favorite food (I'm sure you have many, but pick one for now.). Why do you like it? What can you say about that food that conveys why that food is enjoyable to you? It is not enough, really, to say that you like it "because it tastes good." In this sense, *good* just becomes an empty word that doesn't really say anything.

I like pepperoni pizza. My two favorite places are Angelone's in Portland, Maine, and Burke Street Pizza in Winston-Salem, North Carolina. What I really like is how, on theirs, the slices of pepperoni curl up just a little and get crispy around the edges, leaving a tiny bit of oil residue inside. I also like how their pepperoni slices can easily be bitten into, rather than the big round slabs of pepperoni that some pizzerias use, which sort of slide off whole when you chomp into them, pulling along large segments of cheese. Sure, there are plenty of places that offer adequate pizza, but only rare places like these make pepperoni pizzas that I *really* like.

It is easy (and somewhat distracting!) to come up with details to describe the foods we like; but, what about writing we like? *Why* do we like it? What does it mean to "like" an opening sentence, an image, an insight? Since you don't want to be that student who just jots generic comments down the margins in a hurry, like Ray made a habit of doing, I encourage your class, before workshops even begin, to do an inventory of what makes you like (or dislike) certain features of writing. Not just what makes writing "good," but what makes writing really *work* for us, as individual readers.

Are you a reader who likes detail in the form of facts and data—such as a newspaper article about Dustin Pedroia's injury, one that provides statistics showing how well the Red Sox play when he has been in the line-up compared to their win-loss record without him? Or are you a reader who likes to "discern" by reading in between the lines what an author *might* mean? Do you like to learn about new things, places, people, ideas, when you read, or do you prefer to read about that which is familiar? Do you like writing that makes you feel sadness or frustration, or do you prefer to read stories that look on the brighter side? It is good to know these things about yourself, as you approach any new text.

Now consider this: Is it even possible to *like* the writing that you and your peers have to do for classes? Not always. But, I would argue that you don't have to like the academic writing your peers share with you (i.e., enjoy it the way I enjoy most any article about the Boston Red Sox) in order to praise what's *working* for you as a reader.

Meaningful praise, then, is feedback that recognizes something that is working for you as a reader, that gives you an opportunity to have a dialogue with the author, and that expresses some sort of appreciation for the work the writer has done, or for the writer herself.

I remember when my student who wrote about his football experiences included a detail about coaches making him run up and down the bleachers with garbage bags wrapped tightly around his torso so he could get "in condition" for the upcoming game (I believe this is not allowed anymore). He did not use extensive description or need to. Through one well-chosen detail, he was able to illustrate what the players had to do *and* reveal some of the complexities of being a competitive athlete: his detail allowed the reader to imagine the exhaustion, and to question the methods the coaches used to get some players into shape. Praising the student's use of detail had to involve more than just telling him "nice detail." It meant explaining, as succinctly as I could fit in the margin, what made it work, for me as one reader: "A nice detail. You've already got me appreciating the physical and emotional stress an elite athlete experiences. It must have been draining. How do you feel now about the coaches' methods?" Here is an alternative praise comment, from a peer who likes the passage because he can relate to it: "Good description. Our coaches used to do this too. I like how you make people who don't know what it's like understand what we go through to compete."

Practice Session 1

Let's practice writing praise in response to an actual sample of student writing, the beginning of a personal exploration by Lili Velez. As you read the following excerpt, consider what praise you could write:

Examinations Outside the Classroom

We panic, we pack, we get to college, and then panic again, moaning, "I wish I had known I'd need this!" "This" could be anything from that extra pillow to the answers to a high school test on *Hamlet*, or it might be something more abstract, like how to deal with issues we never thought we would encounter outside a classroom. For example, when a philosophy professor asks us to examine what is evil and what is good, that's okay; we're getting graded on it. But do we ask such questions in the cafeteria? In the dormitory? At home? Who needs to ponder academic questions outside of class? It's an invasion of our private lives. I thought so until a question followed me home and shook up my ideas on what belonged in the classroom and what I should never be without.

It was English 102, in small group discussion of my friend Donna's paper, which was about whether fighting was a natural tendency, as it is in other animals that live in groups. (337)

It would be easy enough to write next to Lili's first paragraph "good opening." It would be simple enough to say that the opening is "descriptive" or "captivating." But, if you like the opening of this essay, what really causes your positive reaction? Even just as a draft, why does this opening *work* for you, as a reader? Take a moment to write two or three sentences describing what it is you like about Lili's writing so far, and imagine you are writing these words directly to her in a conversation.

Is it the word choice? The arrangement of sentences? Her use of detail (the pillow, *Hamlet*)? Does it have something to do with the voice or tone? The way she uses questions? It could be any or all of these things, or something else altogether. I liked the commas and repetition in the first sentence, which create a sense of tension in the writing. (I am the kind of reader who likes some tension in what I read.) I also liked the feeling of momentum. Even just a little bit into the second paragraph, I am curious to hear more about what happened in her small group and the discussion about Donna's paper. As Keith Hjortshoj describes in *The Transition to College Writing*:

> Beginnings are points of departure, when readers expect to learn what this writing is about and the general direction it will take. Even if these beginnings do not explicitly map the routes the writing will travel, they tell us where this journey will start, point us in a certain direction, and provide some bearings for the next move. (115)

Lili is trying to do just that: engage the reader, point us in a specific direction, and pose a central question that will guide the exploration forward.

Elaine Mamon, Lili's instructor in the class, praised Lili for her courage to tackle a challenging topic and for making the reader "feel like getting into the conversation" (Velez 340).

PRACTICE SESSION 2

When writing meaningful praise, you might consider using a technique associated with rhetorician Donald Murray, who was known for writing his praise to students using this format: "I like the way you…" (qtd. in Daiker 111). By including some praise written this way, you help writers enhance their audience awareness. As you read the following excerpt, the opening of a personal essay my student Nick wrote about declining wildlife in Pennsylvania, write 2–3 praise comments in Murray's "I like the way you…" format:

> *Where the Wild Things Roamed*
>
> And there we found ourselves, on my hike in the woods with my dog Loki, his eyes fixed upon a herd of deer who stared back at him with the same intense interest. You could see it stir within them, the ancient war between their kind, Loki likely thinking "Must chase! Must bite!" though he probably does not know why, and the deer screaming in their minds, "The wolf! The wolf!" despite the ironic fact that these deer have never seen a wolf. For there are no wolves in these woods, nor in all of Pennsylvania.

> Gone are the days of wolves and mountain lions prowling through these woods giving the deer something to truly fear rather than this would-be predator at the end of my leash.
>
> And here I am looking at these deer and wondering, "How are you all that's left?" (Brewster 1)

After completing your praise comments, I recommend talking with others in class about what you praised, how you worded each comment, and what it was like writing responses this way.

Donald Daiker believes that writers become less apprehensive when they "experience success" and that "genuine praise can lift the hearts, and the pens, of the writers who sit in our classrooms" (106, 112). After receiving fifteen sets of feedback from his classmates throughout the semester, which all had to include several praise comments, Nick explained his emerging confidence: "I ended up deciding to let my creativity loose despite how uncomfortable it made me. I ended up finding myself greatly enjoying some of my later works. The more confident I became in my writings the more I experimented with my creativity." In one of his final peer comments on a classmate's meta-essay, Nick acknowledges the role positive peer feedback had played in their mutual development: "Great point and I agree. We helped one another write about more personal feelings and dilemmas."

Examples of Peer Response Praise

Let's look at several other praise comments Nick writes on his classmates' essays. For context, most of the papers students wrote in this class revolved around animals, or writing, and sometimes both:

- Repeating the questions was an effective follow-up to your intro sentence
- Nice allusion. Very creative way of describing your writings.

Notice how Nick refers to specific choices the writer had made. Here are some comments Nick writes on Carolyn's essay about six cats she has owned throughout her life. Sometimes, Nick praises Carolyn for the choices she makes as a writer, and sometimes he praises her personally, but all of them are conversational:

- Good details that add to each cat's character
- Interesting how everyone ended up getting their "own" cat

- The font change is a good touch [Carolyn had switched fonts for a passage that recreated a letter she would have written as a child to her cat who had passed away]
- Recognizing how you've changed over time and looking back on your younger self is such a human thing to do and extremely relatable. I think we've all been there.
- Great imagery and comical, picturing this level of organization from a child
- LOL! Nice touch and some comic relief after the passing of Chester

Occasionally, Nick writes what Rick Straub and Ronald Lunsford refer to as combination comments, wherein a praise comment is joined with a question or tentative advice. For example, in response to Jordan's essay about his dog Quinn, Nick writes:

- Good descriptions [of Quinn]. Maybe could add more? Hair type, face, size?

On Rose's essay, which analyzes the effects of a social media influencer who hoards animals (particularly rats and reptiles), Nick combines praise, analysis, and a rhetorical question:

- Good point. It does certainly appear we care about some animals more than others. Would people care more if it was a room full of puppies, for example?

Notice how in responding to Rose's argument, Nick has joined the conversation as a reader. The best peer feedback does not just inflate the writer's ego but keeps the conversation about the writing, and about the topic, moving forward. The praise you receive can help you understand what goes on in your readers' minds, and better shape your writing for an audience.

In his article "Responding—Really Responding—To Other Students' Writing," Straub encourages you to "Challenge yourself to write as many praise comments as criticisms. When you praise, praise well. Sincerity and specificity are everything when it comes to a compliment" (192). Nick includes a good deal of praise in his sets of feedback, and his comments are specific and sincere.

Final Advice and Thoughts

You may try to write your peer response using different color pens—for example, green for praise, orange for combination comments, or green to praise stylistic techniques and blue to praise ideas. Also, give yourself enough space and time to write conversational praise. As an example, Andrea writes in the space next to Jordan's title "The Unwritten": *I really like your title—it fits well with the theme running through about things we must accept in life that are too complicated to be written in a rulebook. Since you only mention writing a couple times in the piece, it's nice and subtle.* In the left margin of Carolyn's essay "Alone," Andrea writes, *I like the repetition of the two phrases "but I am alone" and "my cat who is on my chest." Even though there are multiple metaphors in this piece, keeping the repetition going grounds the reader to where the narrator is and really creates the feeling of what it's like when your body isn't moving but your brain is going a million miles an hour.* Andrea writes small and can fit this comment in the top margin, but you may want to write lengthier praise on the back of the page or in an endnote/letter to the author.

Although it takes a bit more time to write such conversational praise, compared to "Good title," or "I like the repetition," Andrea's comments say so much more to Jordan and Carolyn. They are examples of what Donald Daiker would describe as "genuine praise" (112).

Being a peer responder is not just about being a good one or a bad one, it is, just as it is with your writing, about your investment in joining a real conversation with others. When combined with additional types of peer feedback that you will practice—such as asking questions, giving advice for revision, critiquing an argument's shortcomings, and/or making corrections—praising well and with sincerity will help your classmates improve their writing and enhance their desire to write with a specific audience in mind. Together, you will avoid "the descent" and develop as writers and readers, and maybe even enjoy the journey together.

Works Cited

Brewster, Nick. "Where the Wild Things Roamed." 18 March 2019. EN3090: Writing About Animals, Delaware Valley University, student paper.

Daiker, Donald. "Learning to Praise." *Writing and Response: Theory, Practice, Research*, edited by Chris Anson, NCTE, 1989, pp. 103-113.

Hjortshoj, Keith. *The Transition to College Writing*, 2nd ed., Bedford, 2009.

Velez, Lili. "Examinations Outside the Classroom." *What Makes Writing Good: A Multiperspective*, edited by William Coles and James Vopat, D.C. Heath, 1985, pp. 337-339.

Mamon, Elaine. "Commentary." *What Makes Writing Good: A Multiperspective*, edited by William Coles and James Vopat, D.C. Heath, 1985, pp. 339-342.

Sobchack, Vivian. "On (Not) Watching Horror: Looking Awry at *The Descent* and *Isolation*." *Film Comment*, vol. 42, 2006, pp. 38-41.

Straub, Richard. "Responding—Really Responding—To Other Students' Writing." *The Subject is Writing*, 4th ed., edited by Wendy Bishop and James Strickland, Boynton/Cook, 2006, pp. 187-197.

Straub, Richard and Ronald Lunsford. *Twelve Readers Reading: Responding to College Student Writing*, Hampton, 1995.

Teacher Resources for How to Write Meaningful Peer Response Praise by Ron DePeter

Introduction for Teachers

Instructors could assign this essay in a first-year or upper-level writing course or workshop, during the early part of a semester when students are practicing peer feedback. The essay is in some sense an indirect sequel to Straub's "Response—Really Responding—To Other Students' Writing," looking more in-depth at one specific mode of peer response. It is recommended that students have opportunities to practice writing feedback—perhaps on one or more sample essays that the instructor has collected from previous students. Ideally, students should practice writing each mode of commentary (for example, 1–2 sessions writing praise, 1–2 sessions writing questions/advice, 1–2 sessions combining several modes) before diving into small group or whole class workshops. Ideally, the instructor can give some feedback or grades on the practice feedback, letting the students know how they are doing and how they might improve (e.g., write more comments, make comments more specific, etc.). After each peer feedback practice session, and in the "real" workshops with classmates, students can reflect in their journal/class discussion on how they feel they are coming along as responders, as well as how they feel about the comments received. Such meta-writings are essential threads that facilitate the students' growth as readers and responders.

Discussion Questions

1. Do any of the attitudes about peer response that DePeter discusses in the beginning of his essay apply to you (e.g., not wanting to "judge" others or regarding a teacher's feedback as more important than peers')? Where do you imagine these attitudes come from?
2. How do you think Nick (or any peer) would feel hearing the praise comments written in the Donald Murray style of "I like the way you…"? What effect would such praise have on the writer, compared to just seeing "Good" next to a passage?
3. Do you feel there is a difference between what you feel is "good writing," and that which teachers have identified as "good?" If so, what accounts for these different expectations? What is your definition of "good writing?"

4. Can you think of ways that Nick or Andrea's peer response praise could be even sharper, or more helpful to an author?
5. Discuss experiences you have had in other classes sharing peer response. Have they been a metaphorical *"Descent,"* or enjoyable journeys? What made your peer response sessions in the past work, or not work?

4 Writing with Force and Flair

William T. FitzGerald

Overview

Exposure to rhetorical figures, once central to writing pedagogy, has largely fallen out of favor in composition. This chapter reintroduces today's students to the stylistic possibilities of figures of speech, drawing on an analogy to figure skating to illustrate how writing communicates with an audience through stylistic moves. In an accessible discussion of how and why to use figures, it provides an overview of the most common tropes (e.g., metaphor, hyperbole) and schemes (e.g. isocolon, anaphora) and offers brief definitions and examples to illustrate their variety and ubiquity. It discusses the situated nature of writing to acknowledge that while even academic writing employs rhetorical figures, not all figures are appropriate for every genre and context. The essay concludes with a set of style-based exercises to supplement a writing course. These include maintaining a commonplace book, analyzing texts, imitating passages, and practicing techniques of copia for stylistic flexibility. Some resources are recommended for further study.

If you watch figure skaters in the Winter Olympics, the only time I really do, you know the athleticism and artistry of these competitors.* You see it in their faces, in their bodies, in the way they fearlessly "attack" the ice. You can only marvel at the hours of practice and the slow accumulation of technical mastery required to make it all seem so effortless. Watching figure skating on TV, I always notice the commentary. The presenters speak a language incomprehensible to me to describe what we see. A double *this*, a triple *that*, a reverse *something-or-other*. All *I* see is

---

* This work is licensed under the Creative Commons Attribution-NonCommercial-NoDerivatives 4.0 International License (CC BY-NC-ND 4.0) and are subject to the Writing Spaces Terms of Use. To view a copy of this license, visit http://creativecommons.org/licenses/by-nc-nd/4.0/, email info@creativecommons.org, or send a letter to Creative Commons, PO Box 1866, Mountain View, CA 94042, USA. To view the Writing Spaces Terms of Use, visit http://writingspaces.org/terms-of-use.

skaters looking elegant as they weave intricate moves into beautiful and inspiring performances.

Writing, I think, is not unlike skating (or cooking or painting or piloting an airplane). Each of these activities may be learned and taught. Writing is one skill that, with sufficient "ice time," it is possible to do passably well. Recently, I have thought about writing's relation to skating in another way: in the connection between figure *skating* and the so-called figures of *speech*. I believe there are useful analogies between the twists and turns that skaters perform on the ice and the moves writers perform on the page. This essay makes a case for *figurative* language as indispensable to effective writing. I hope it helps to show how you can write with force and flair.

Every field has its share of technical terms for critical tools and concepts. While outsiders are often reduced to using "doohickey" or "thingamabob," insiders know the differences among families of related terms. Every plumber knows her wrenches (e.g., monkey, socket, Allen). Italian cooks have intimate knowledge of pasta shapes (e.g., linguine, rigatoni). The same can be said of the many rhetorical devices of style for speaking and writing, including terms you already know such as *alliteration* (repeated sounds at the beginning of words (e.g., "*c*lear and *c*onvincing evidence"). Fortunately, you don't need to know the name of every figure to use them well.

At the same time, even modest exposure to some as yet unfamiliar terms for quite familiar features of language can help you develop a sense of what is possible in your writing. And knowing a range of *rhetorical figures* has a tangible benefit: you allow yourself to use more "whatchamacallits" in your writing because you realize they *can* be used. Literally hundreds of rhetorical figures—from *antimetabole* to *zeugma*—have been catalogued over time, beginning in ancient Greece and Rome. However, it is unlikely you will have reason to learn many of these figures by name. But it is important to realize that you *already* use them, or at least admire them. *Antimetabole*? From the Greek, meaning a change in direction, this is a reversal of word order for instructive or ironic effect, as in "We should eat to live, not live to eat." Or, in the words of Malcolm X, "We didn't land on Plymouth Rock... Plymouth rock landed on us." (232). And *Zeugma*? Also from the Greek, meaning to tie together, that's the use of a single word to join two or more unrelated words or ideas, as in "He *lost* his keys and his temper" or "You are *beautiful* inside and out." Typically, we only notice this figure when there is a difference in how a single word is used, as here with two senses of *lost*—a literal sense and a figural sense.

When I introduce such figures to my students, they wish they had learned more about them earlier. In that spirit of curiosity, then, I offer a brief tour of rhetorical figures you might wish to incorporate into your writing, give some concrete advice to help you get started, and end with some resources to help you learn more about the figures on your own.

Trying Out Tropes, Sorting Out Schemes

The so-called figures of speech occupy a place in oratory and in writing at once central and marginal. Today, virtually every handbook of writing recognizes three "virtues" of style: clarity, correctness, and appropriateness. In classical times, however, and well into the nineteenth century, a fourth virtue of "ornament" was also recognized. It is to this category of ornament that the figures, in all their variety, belong. We might think of ornament as decoration or adornment, but originally *ornatus* meant something closer to furnished or well-equipped. Rhetorical figures, then, may be likened to the gear one carries as if in battle, on hand for when needed. They're a Swiss army knife for words.

For a better sense of how rhetorical figures equip you to write with force and flair, it helps to recognize that "figure" has two overlapping senses: *expression* and *pattern*. In the first sense, figures are expressions at the level of word or phrase that deviate from ordinary or expected meaning. These include figures of speech such as metaphor and irony. These types of figures are also known as *tropes*. A trope (from the Greek, meaning "turn," hence a turn of phrase) involves a substitution of one word or phrase for another or related word play. For instance, we may use "lion-hearted" as a metaphor for courage or "chicken" as its opposite. (In fact, "courage" comes from the French for heart.) Some other tropes you have likely encountered are *personification* (assigning human qualities to animals or inanimate objects, as in "Fortune smiled on us") and *hyperbole* (exaggerated speech, as in "I've told you a million times!").

Other rhetorical figures involve language that stands out for its shape. These are called *schemes*, verbal expressions that involve repetition, contrast, omission, or reversal of typical word order. Schemes (from the Greek, for "pattern") generally occur at levels beyond the word and sometimes the sentence. They serve to structure ideas and to strengthen arguments. Indeed, if a figure of speech isn't serving to advance an argument, it's not really doing its job.

We typically think of figures as verbal moves that give distinction to our prose. Consider the memorable exhortation by President Kennedy in his inaugural address: "And so my fellow Americans, ask not what your country can do for you--ask what you can do for your country" (270). This famous sentence once again employs the figure of *antimetabole*. One of a handful of figures that invert sentence elements, this particular instance reinforces underlying calls for a new spirit of patriotism and public service. The sentence is not just a memorable turn of phrase—one way to understand figures—here the *form* of expression argues for a different way to think about the relationship between a government and its citizens. Try to imagine other ways to state this idea, and it becomes clear how powerful Kennedy's phrasing is. More than standing out, figures do the heavy lifting. In contemporary language, figures are like verbal "apps" we download to our stylistic repertoire.

You might notice that I used a figure to discuss figures, specifically, the device of *simile* to compare one thing (figures) with another (digital tools). *Simile* (from the Greek for "likeness") is perhaps the most common trope, together with its cousin *metaphor* (to use a metaphor of family resemblance). Note, too, that these two figures perform basic functions of thought through analogy. In other words, m*etaphor* and *simile* are not just optional add-ons expressing what might otherwise be said in a literal, as opposed to a figurative, way. Rather, they *are* the very thoughts we express to make sense of things for ourselves and for others. Because they are so basic to thinking and communicating, figures well up to the surface naturally. They are recognizable enough and common enough to be given a name and to be used intentionally. But before they become lists of devices, they are first in our minds and in our speech.

Sometimes an idea bounces around in our brains, *wanting* to be a figure. Take the scheme of *polyptoton* (Greek for "many cases"), in which the same root word is repeated in different forms or parts of speech, such as *lose* (verb), *lost* (adjective), *loser* (noun) over one or more sentences. Or in a tight expression like "*Fight* the good *fight*." Generated more or less by accident, often, these variations can be used more or less on purpose to shape material and to move minds. Figures become a strategy where used deliberately. For example, I used a *metaphor* "well up to the surface" to understand how a thought finds expression at the level of the sentence. In fact, as I was writing this paragraph I was hoping a metaphor might suggest itself to show how figures are both *naturally discovered* as well as *deliberately employed*. (Note the scheme of *parallelism* in the previous sentence?)

Indeed, metaphors and other figures are hard to avoid. They come to us as much as we to them. Yet we may find ourselves pushing them away, perhaps in the belief that they are inappropriate for a given audience, purpose, or genre. This is especially the case in academic writing, where we want to avoid sounding verbose or "flowery." (The figures are also known as the "flowers of rhetoric.") But even academic and professional writing uses tropes like *metaphor* and schemes like *parallelism* to communicate, argue, and persuade. It can be as simple as using multiple words with similar endings (e.g., educa*tion*, compensa*tion*) while avoiding obvious rhymes (e.g., *rosy*, *nosy*). All writing has a context that brings creative pressure to bear on our choice of stylistic tools.

When we write, we must be open to figures that suggest themselves. Like the use of wild yeast to start a dough in artisanal baking, our use of figures is largely a matter of letting things happen naturally, at first, and later being willing to "knead the dough" with our hands. For example, in the previous paragraph, I used both balance and repetition to pair "more or less by accident" with "more or less on purpose." In truth, I did so *more or less* by accident. Initially, the phrasing came to me. I wanted to contrast inspiration (wild yeast metaphor) and intention (kneading metaphor) by using parallel phrasing to set off contrasting ideas. (This is the scheme of *antithesis*.) After first writing "deliberately," I later chose "on purpose" to highlight the parallelism.

I was also aware that this particular use of phrases of equal length was an instance of *isocolon* (Greek for "of same length"). These figures of parallel construction at the level of word, phrase or even clause are perhaps the most common scheme to signify relationships between two or more things. They take *some* effort but are not especially exotic. For another example of *isocolon*, refer back to the heading for this section: Trying Out Tropes, Sorting Out Schemes.) At times, balanced expressions take the form of a logical or temporal progression, as in the famous *tricolon* of Julius Caesar describing victory in the Gallic wars: "Veni, vidi, vinci" ("I came; I saw; I conquered."). Or consider Abraham Lincoln's immortal use of this same figure in the Gettysburg Address: "government *of the people, by the people, for the people* shall not perish from the earth" (Lincoln).

Too Noticeable? How Much is Too Much?

As I have said, no use of figures, no aspect of writing, can be assessed apart from its context. To some audiences, a metaphor will seem far-fetched, the injection of irony ineffective. Does my analogy of writing to figure skating work for you? Does my characterization of figures as verbal "apps" strike you as appropriate for this essay? These are the kinds of questions you must consider whenever you use tropes or schemes to bring your material to life before an audience. The better we know our audience, purpose, and genre, the more likely we are to select effective "verbal" apps. When we are less confident, we reign in our figurative imagination, choose to play it straight.

If we are not careful, writing with force and flare comes across as mere show—in the useful figure of *cliché,* all hat and no cattle. Or as any cook can tell you, a *little* nutmeg goes a long way. To extend this culinary analogy, rhetorical figures may be likened to a spice rack, without which writing cannot be anything but bland. What is needed is the right *combination* of spices as a matter of both taste and tradition. Different occasions call for different types and degrees of figuration. What may work in a personal essay does not necessarily work in a research report.

Verbal style ranges from very simple to highly ornate. Ornamental writing draws attention to itself as well as to its subject matter. In doing so, it pronounces an attitude about its subject, maybe solemn or perhaps irreverent. Our writing may risk seeming overly poetic or sounding too much like oratory.

Many students, I have noticed, are fond of the *rhetorical question* as a device for inciting a reader's interest. It's true that this move can be something of a crutch, since it's easier to ask a series of questions than to state a claim outright. Despite that risk, I encourage my students to consider posing a question at times to focus their readers' attention and to let readers know that the writer is thinking of them, interacting with them. Many scholars of rhetoric distinguish such interactive devices as *rhetorical questions* from the two categories of tropes and schemes we have already identified. These so-called *figures of thought* (in contrast to *figures of speech*) include the technique of *anticipating objections* (in Greek, prolepsis), such as "I know what you are going to say, but hear me out." Most effective writing consists of well-reasoned arguments *and* a range of figurative devices to deliver those points efficiently and elegantly.

Likewise, I encourage my students to consider the powerful scheme of *anaphora,* although sparingly. *Anaphora* (from the Greek meaning "to carry back") is repetition at the beginning of successive phrases clauses, or sentences. Here again is Lincoln in the Gettysburg Address: "But in a larger sense, *we cannot* dedicate, *we cannot* consecrate, *we cannot* hallow this ground" (Lincoln 23). Here, Lincoln's repeated use of "we cannot" in successive clauses gives solemnity to a speech honoring the dead, but it also reinforces his argument that "we," the living, must turn from mourning to the task of seeing that the dead did not die in vain.

When I survey my students, they admit reluctance to use *anaphora* or other figures of repetition, worried they will be faulted for being repetitive. Given that all writing is contextual, I cannot say I blame them. But *anaphora* and related figures of repetition should always be in your toolkit of possible figures. Intentional repetition is different from haphazard redundancy. Readers like knowing they are in the good hands of writers who have thought carefully about what they want to do in their writing.

Especially, I tell my students that as we write, we must also listen. Most writing that we admire brings the immediacy of sound to the page, including through rhetorical devices that appeal as much to the ear as to the eye. The deliberate use of sound-based devices like *alliteration* (repeated sounds at the beginning of words) and, of course, *rhyme* (repeated sounds at the end of words) can be the difference between a *s*erviceable *s*entence and a *s*pectacular one. Okay, I suppose rhyme is one figure we should think twice about using in academic contexts, but we should never rule it out entirely.

On the whole, I believe that we must overcome a long-standing suspicion about the use of rhetorical figures, a suspicion that we inherited from the so-called Age of Reason. In this historical period following the Renaissance—a high-water mark for ornament—figurative language fell into disrepute. Because of their recognized effects on emotions, the figures came to be regarded as *too* persuasive, appropriate for advertising rhetoric but not academic writing, the stuff of poetry rather than prose. This bias is a major reason why the figures, although once taught to every student, are now more likely encountered in the study of literature than in the writing classroom. In general, you have not been encouraged to incorporate such devices into your writing. Perhaps it's time to try?

Go Figure

In a course I have taught several times entitled "Go Figure," my students learn about style through hands-on attention to tropes and schemes. Based on my experience, I highlight four practices you can do in or out of any writing course, including first year composition. Each of these activities prepares you to write with force and flair, whether in an academic paper or in some other context.

Fieldwork

One way to learn about something is to gather specimens. Like pressed flowers, figures found in various places can be assembled into a commonplace book or, as here, a "figure journal." I recommend one or two entries a week in a semester-long course. Each entry, on its own page, is an example of a figure identified, defined, and analyzed for its effects. By collecting your examples, you discover just how many "real world" instances of tropes and schemes are to be found. In a classroom, each student might have a turn presenting a figure. This fun project cements knowledge of figures and their terms. It's a fascinating way to see that figures identified more than two thousand years ago, in different languages, are alive and well today in English.

ANALYSIS

To see which figures appear in various genres and contexts, you can analyze texts of interest to you. Some may be rich in tropes, others in schemes. Comparing academic and popular writing or fiction and non-fiction can give you a perspective on tone and stylistic tools. Select several passages to analyze and try to identify as many figures as you can, looking for any patterns to emerge. You might examine several texts in the same genre or different texts by the same author. Ask yourself, what accounts for the presence or absence of particular figures? How do audience and purpose influence the use of figures? Time spent in close reading of this kind can have a very positive effect on your own writing.

IMITATION

Paying close attention to other writers can lead to outright imitation. If analysis is good, imitation is better. Since classical times, students have copied passages, word for word, to get inside writing they, or their teachers, admire. They then produce a close imitation. In my "Go Figure" course, we choose short passages to imitate, just a sentence or two, usually with a particularly distinctive or ornate style. Everyone first copies the passages, pen in hand, to get a feel for each sentence. We then attempt a phrase-by-phrase imitation, putting new content into the existing sentence structure. Comparing our individual responses to this exercise is both enlightening and entertaining. A weekly imitation exercise like this has a cumulative effect of helping you internalize figurative devices and learn the flow of sentences.

COPIA (PLENTY)

In contemporary approaches to writing and writing instruction, a certain economy of expression leaves many rhetorical options off the table. Many of us have internalized values of brevity and efficiency that discourage letting our words run wild, even when drafting. We don't tolerate more words than are strictly necessary. But writing with a feel for figures encourages strategies of *copia* (plenty), that is, having more things to say and more ways to say a thing. The most famous account of copious writing was composed five hundred years ago by Dutch scholar Desiderius Erasmus in his popular textbook of 1512, *De Copia*. Erasmus championed stylistic fluency to achieve an abundant style and recommended a valuable exercise: write a sentence in many, many ways. As an example, Erasmus offers 195 variations, all in Latin, on a base sentence, "Your letter pleased me mightily" (348) To reach that high number, Erasmus employs a wide range of synonyms—*missive* or *epistle* for *letter, delighted* for *pleased*—but also many figures of speech, chiefly tropes that substitute one word or phrase for another. These include *metaphor*: "Your communication *poured vials of joy on my head*" (349); *synecdoche* (substituting part for whole): "Your *lines* [for entire letter] conveyed to me the greatest joy" (349); and *metonymy* (associated thing): "To be sure your letter delighted *my spirits* [for me]!" (349). Another instance of *metonymy* refers to the *hand* that wrote the letter: "I was in no small measure refreshed in spirit by your grace's hand" (349). Erasmus also uses the interesting figure of *litotes*, a kind of understatement by negation: "Your epistle afforded me *no small delight*" (349). In our course, "Go Figure," we experimented with producing 50 to 100 variations of a base sentence, trying to use as many figures as we could. Try this, and there's no question you will learn the ins and outs of writing by performing these sentence sit-ups.

Each of these practices of compiling, analyzing, imitating, and varying offers something of value. They can be part of any writing class in small bursts alongside formal writing. Of course, this ongoing practice leads to a final practice: using rhetorical devices yourself in actual papers. In the past, I have asked my students to incorporate and identify figures of their own, say six or more in a four to five page paper. This expectation encourages experimentation in drafting and revising, since all texts present opportunities for ornamentation as they take shape.

Another word for experimentation is *play*. My approach recognizes the value of play. Too often, we focus on clarity and correctness to the exclusion of other virtues. Not that we shouldn't value being clear and error-free in our writing. It's just that we can also write, as I say, with force and flair. Even academic writing is not a "figure-free" zone. While I cannot guarantee that using figures will allow you to "skate through" a writing course, I can promise that *figure* skating through composition will make your writing both more enjoyable and more impactful.

It is through ornament in your choice and arrangement of words that readers relate to your writing. It is through ornament that *you* relate to your writing. To return to the ice once more, figures are best understood as the glides, pivots, jumps, and spins by which you communicate what you really want to say to your audience. Through figures subtle and bold, you communicate attitude, passion, dedication to craft, expertise, respect for your audience and your subject.

So give it a whirl!

Learn More about Rhetorical Figures

Throughout this essay, I have referenced a handful or two of the most common tropes (e.g., metaphor, synecdoche) and schemes (e.g., anaphora, isocolon) to give you a sense of both how they work and how widespread they are. At the same time, I have not tried to identify *all* the figures, let alone explain them in detail. I hope I piqued your interest enough that you will learn more about them on your own or with the help of your teacher.

Just as there are dozens of figures, there are many Web sites and books that explain and catalog figures of speech. I note two Web sites in particular:

- For a clear overview and comprehensive account of figurative language from a respected academic source, consult *Silva Rhetoricae* (The Forest of Rhetoric), hosted by Gideon Burton of Brigham Young University. There you will find multiple pages breaking down figures into categories beyond just tropes and schemes.
- For a comical and quirky take on figurative language in everyday life, check out Jay Heinrich's *Figures of Speech Served Fresh*. For ten years, Heinrich (aka Figaro) posted witty essays drawing from politics, literature, and popular culture to show that figurative language is indeed everywhere.

Either of these sites will boost your confidence to welcome the figures into your writing.

Questions for Discussion

1. Which figures in this essay or elsewhere do you want to experiment with in your writing?

2. What figures in writing by others do you admire and wish to emulate? After reading this essay, can you better recognize figurative devices, if not necessarily by name?
3. What can you learn about writing as a craft from Erasmus' exercise in *copia*? How could you push past 50, 100, or even 200 variations?
4. What rhetorical figures are appropriate for academic writing? What rhetorical figures are inappropriate for academic writing? What borderline cases can you identify for particular figures?
5. Now that you know a little more about rhetorical figures, can you identify any that seem to be part of your stylistic tool kit in your everyday writing, perhaps on social media?

Works Cited

Erasmus, Desiderius. *Copia: Foundations of the Abundant Style*. Translated by Betty I. Knott. *Collected Works of Erasmus*, vol. 24, edited by Craig R Thompson, University of Toronto P, 1978, pp. 348-354.

Kennedy, John F. "Inaugural Address." Washington, D.C. 20 Jan. 1961. *The Presidents Speak: The Inaugural Addresses of the American Presidents from Washington to Kennedy*, edited by Davis Newton Lott, Holt, Rinehart and Winston, 1961, pp. 269-271.

Lincoln, Abraham. "Address Delivered at the Dedication of the Cemetery at Gettysburg, Final Text." 19 Nov. 1863. *The Collected Works of Abraham Lincoln*, vol. 7, edited by Roy P. Basler, Rutgers UP, 1955, pp. 23.

X, Malcolm. *The Autobiography of Malcolm X*. 1965. Edited by Alex Haley, Ballantine Books, 2015.

Teacher Resources for Writing with Force and Flair by William T. FitzGerald

Overview and Teaching Strategies

This essay on the use of rhetorical figures is ideally taught as part of a general approach to writing, and writing in college contexts, as a means for exploring attitudes, expectations, and presumed restrictions that students (and, often, teachers) may bring to the composition classroom. It is intended to start conversation and spark interest in experimenting with the resources of stylistic figuration.

Students will typically know a handful of rhetorical figures by name (alliteration, onomatopoeia) based on exposure to literary devices in previous English (literature) classes. But they are not likely to think of rhetorical figures as tools they can use in *their* writing. This chapter encourages exactly that, but unless students are given permission, encouragement even, from their instructor, they are unlikely to follow up on this invitation.

A challenge in teaching this essay is anchoring it to exercises in language exploration and play, as suggested in the section "Go Figure" and below. A second challenge is supplementing a reading of the chapter together with further discussion and examples. Figurative language is everywhere, from puns and sound-based features of spoken and written prose to punctuation effects in digital environments. Indeed, there are likely new figures.

A final challenge is one this author has wrestled with personally with his students. How much Greek and Roman nomenclature is too much? There is no question that learning a catalog of rhetorical figures is overwhelming and arguably beside the point of the essay. What's more important is to teach patterns and options rather than assimilate a list of strange-sounding names. At the same time, it's useful to recognize these established moves have names—and a long lineage. So long as students know they won't be tested on their recall of specific figures, it's useful to call the figures by their names when exploring their features and functions.

Questions

1. Which figures in this essay or elsewhere do you want to experiment with in your writing?
2. What figures in writing by others do you admire and wish to emulate? After reading this essay, can you better recognize figurative devices, if not necessarily by name?

3. What can you learn about writing as a craft from Erasmus' exercise in *copia*? How could you push past 50, 100, or even 200 variations?
4. What rhetorical figures are appropriate for academic writing? What rhetorical figures are inappropriate for academic writing? What borderline cases can you identify for particular figures?
5. Now that you know a little more about rhetorical figures, can you identify any that seem to you to be part of your stylistic tool kit in your everyday writing, perhaps on social media?

Activities

This essay ends with brief descriptions of four exercises that have been part of courses I have taught on style or figures of speech in particular: compiling a figure journal, analyzing texts, imitating passages, practicing copia. It's probably not prudent to include all of these exercises in a single semester of first year writing. One or two, carefully scaffolded and sustained, seems a productive sidebar addition to a first year writing course. Those identified here are intended as models to be adapted to local situations. This essay and related exercises should be introduced early in a semester, around the time of a first paper draft or revision.

Hands-on attention to style and figuration meets students as readers and writers in unexpected ways to boost awareness of rhetorical aspects of writing. Rather than see prose as a neutral vehicle for expressing ideas, students can learn to notice elements of design and infer intended effects. Such insights can thus transfer to their own writing. But do not expect an immediate impact on the writing that students do. Confidence in employing figures does not come easily.

A final activity, then, is to encourage students to experiment with rhetorical figures in their own papers. Students might be asked, per the questions above, if there are particular figures they would want to use in a future writing project. They might also be asked to identify a handful of figures they find themselves using, whether by design or fortuitously.

5 An Introduction to and Strategies for Multimodal Composing

Melanie Gagich

Overview

This chapter introduces multimodal composing and offers five strategies for creating a multimodal text. The essay begins with a brief review of key terms associated with multimodal composing and provides definitions and examples of the five modes of communication. The first section of the essay also introduces students to the New London Group and offers three reasons why students should consider multimodal composing an important skill—one that should be learned in a writing class. The second half of the essay offers three pre-drafting and two drafting strategies for multimodal composing. Pre-drafting strategies include urging students to consider their rhetorical situation, analyze other multimodal texts, research textual content, gather visual and aural materials, and evaluate tools needed for creating their text. A brief discussion of open licenses and Creative Commons licenses is also included. Drafting strategies include citing and attributing various types of texts appropriately and suggesting that students begin drafting with an outline, script, or visual (depending on the project). I conclude the chapter with suggestions for further reading.

When you think about a college writing class, you probably think of pens, paper, word processors, printers, and, of course, essay writing.* However, on the first day of your college writing class, you might read the syllabus and notice that the first assignment asks you to create a "multimodal text." You may wonder to yourself, "What

---

* This work is licensed under the Creative Commons Attribution-NonCommercial-NoDerivatives 4.0 International License (CC BY-NC-ND 4.0) and are subject to the Writing Spaces Terms of Use. To view a copy of this license, visit http://creativecommons.org/licenses/by-nc-nd/4.0/, email info@creativecommons.org, or send a letter to Creative Commons, PO Box 1866, Mountain View, CA 94042, USA. To view the Writing Spaces Terms of Use, visit http://writingspaces.org/terms-of-use.

does multimodal mean?" Perhaps you remember an assignment from high school when your teacher required you to create a Prezi or PowerPoint presentation, and she referred to it as a "multimodal project," but you were not exactly sure what that meant. Or perhaps you only remember writing five paragraph essays in high school and have never heard or read the word "multimodal."

As a first-year and upper-level composition instructor who has integrated a multimodal project into my curriculums since 2014, I have encountered many questions and confusion related to multimodal composing, or what is sometimes referred to as "multimodality." While some students are thrilled to compose something other than an academic essay, others struggle to understand why they are required to create a multimodal text in a writing class. I assure my students that although they may not be familiar with the concept of multimodality, it has a long history in composition (e.g. writing studies). In fact, the "multimodal assignment" has been a fixture in some college writing classrooms for over a decade and continues to be prevalent in many classrooms. In light of the probability that you will be asked to create a multimodal text at some point in your academic and/or professional career, I wrote this chapter to help you understand and navigate multimodal composing. In the first half of this chapter, I provide brief definitions of terms associated with and explain the importance of multimodal composing. The remainder of the chapter offers strategies for composing a multimodal text with an emphasis on pre-drafting strategies.

What Is a Multimodal Text?

Before moving into a discussion of multimodality and modes of communication, it is important to understand the meaning of the word "text" because it is often only associated with writing (or perhaps the messages you receive or write on your phone). However, when we use the term "text" in composition courses, we often mean it is a piece of communication that can take many forms. For instance, a text is a movie, meme, social media post, essay, website, podcast, and the list goes on. In our daily lives, we encounter, interact with, and consume many types of texts, and it is important to consider how most texts are also multimodal.

Pamela Takayoshi and Cynthia L. Selfe, two important scholars in writing studies and early advocates of multimodal composing, define multimodal texts as "texts that exceed the alphabetical and may include still and moving images, animators, color, words, music, and sound" (1). You'll notice that the examples of "text" listed above are also multimodal, which demonstrates how often we encounter multimodality in our daily lives. Multimodality is sometimes associated with technology and/or digital writing spaces. For example, when you post an image to Instagram, you use technology (your phone) to snap a picture, an app to edit or modify the image, and a social media platform (Instagram) to share it with others. However, creating a multimodal text does not require the use of digital tools and/or does not need to be shared in online digital spaces to make it "multimodal." To illustrate, when you create a collage and post it on your dorm room door, you use existing printed artifacts such as pictures clipped and pasted (non-digital technologies) from a magazine and share with others by taping it to your door (a non-digital space). Both examples represent a multimodal text because they include various modes of communication.

THE FIVE MODES OF COMMUNICATION

In the mid-1990s, a group of scholars gathered in New London, New Hampshire and, based on their discussions, wrote the influential article, "A Pedagogy of Multiliteracies: Designing Social Futures," published in 1996. In it, the group advocated for teachers to embrace teaching practices that allow students to draw from five socially and culturally situated modes, or "way[s] of communicating" (Arola, Sheppard, and Ball 1). These modes were linguistic, visual, spatial, gestural, and aural. Yet, scholars such as Claire Lauer, another influential researcher in composition, have argued that the New London Group's definition of modes, while exceedingly important, can be difficult to grasp. In light of this, below I provide brief definitions of each mode as well as examples to help you understand the "mode" in "multimodal."

WHAT ARE THE MODES OF COMMUNICATION?

The visual mode refers to what an audience can see, such as moving and still images, colors, and alphabetical text size and style. Social media photos (see figure 1) exemplify the visual mode.

Figure 1. Photo of my dog taken from my Facebook page that represents the visual mode.

The linguistic mode refers to alphabetic text or spoken word. Its emphasis is on language and how words are used (verbally or written). A traditional five paragraph essay relies on the linguistic mode; however, this mode is also apparent in some digital texts. Figure 2 shows a student's linguistic text included in their website created to promote game-based language learning.

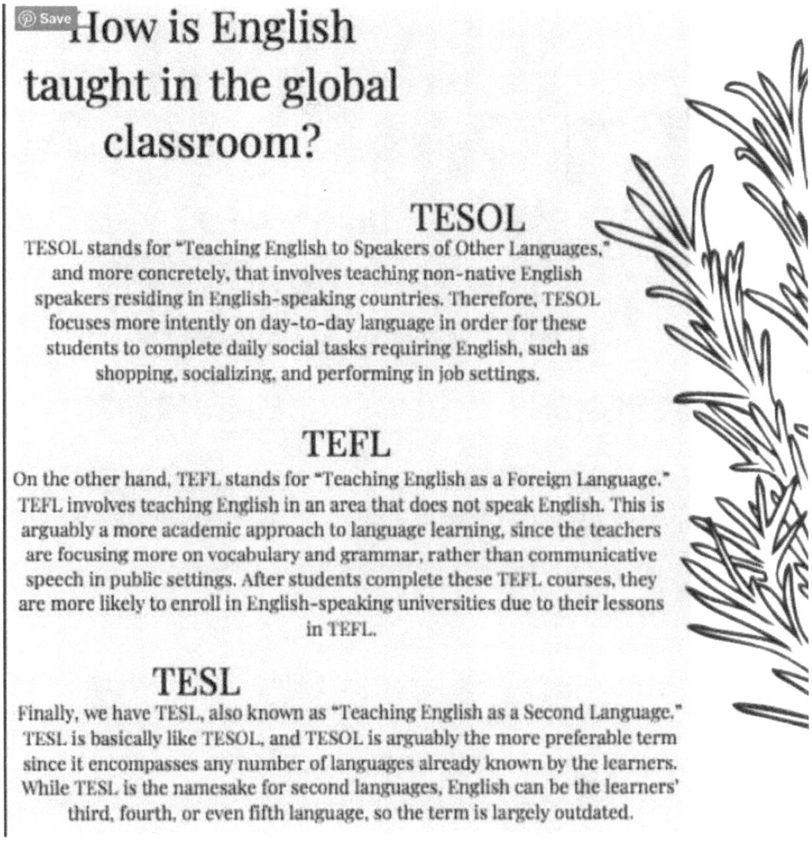

How is English taught in the global classroom?

TESOL
TESOL stands for "Teaching English to Speakers of Other Languages," and more concretely, that involves teaching non-native English speakers residing in English-speaking countries. Therefore, TESOL focuses more intently on day-to-day language in order for these students to complete daily social tasks requiring English, such as shopping, socializing, and performing in job settings.

TEFL
On the other hand, TEFL stands for "Teaching English as a Foreign Language." TEFL involves teaching English in an area that does not speak English. This is arguably a more academic approach to language learning, since the teachers are focusing more on vocabulary and grammar, rather than communicative speech in public settings. After students complete these TEFL courses, they are more likely to enroll in English-speaking universities due to their lessons in TEFL.

TESL
Finally, we have TESL, also known as "Teaching English as a Second Language." TESL is basically like TESOL, and TESOL is arguably the more preferable term since it encompasses any number of languages already known by the learners. While TESL is the namesake for second languages, English can be the learners' third, fourth, or even fifth language, so the term is largely outdated.

Figure 2. A student's digital text that emphasizes the linguistic mode. Photo shows a Pinterest pin that uses text to briefly explain the differences among TESOL, TEFL, and TESL. Permission to use this image was obtained from the student.

The spatial mode refers to how a text deals with space. This also relates to how other modes are arranged, organized, emphasized, and contrasted in a text. Figure 3, an infographic, is an example of the spatial mode in use because it emphasizes certain percentages and words to achieve its goal.

Figure 3. Infographic emphasizing the spatial mode. The infographic uses different sizes of text and different shapes to emphasize statistics surrounding cancer diagnoses and common types. ("Cancer Infographic" by CDC Global licensed under CC BY 2.0)

The gestural mode refers to gesture and movement. This mode is often apparent in delivery of speeches in the way(s) that speakers move their hands and fix their facial features and in other texts that capture movement such as videos, movies, and television. Figure 4 shows Michelle Obama's gestures at a speech she gave in London.

Figure 4. Picture taken of Michelle Obama while giving a speech that captures the gestural mode. She is standing at a microphone, looking out into the audience, and smiling with her hands clasped against her heart. ("US First Lady, Michelle Obama, speaking at Mulberry School for Girls, London" by DFID licensed under CC BY 2.0)

The aural mode refers to what an audience member can or cannot hear. Music is the most obvious representation of the aural mode, but an absence of sound (silence) is also aural. Examples of texts that emphasize the aural mode include podcasts, music videos, concerts, television series, movies, and radio talk shows. Figure 5 is a screenshot of my student's podcast created to convince teachers to integrate podcasts into their language arts classrooms. A podcast exemplifies the aural mode because of its reliance on sound.

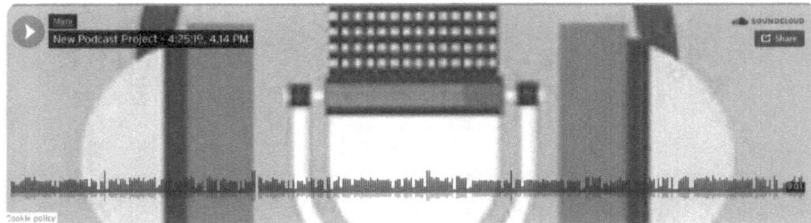

Figure 5 is a screen shot of a student's podcast and shows the audio lines and length of the text, entitled "New Podcast Project." (Permission to use this image was obtained from the student).

A multimodal text combines various modes of communication (hence the combination of the words "multiple" and "mode" in the term "multimodal"). Cheryl E. Ball and Colin Charlton draw from The New London Group in their argument that "[a]ny combination of modes makes a multimodal text, and all text—every piece of communication a human composes—use more than one mode. Thus, all writing is multimodal" (42). However, in some communicative texts, one mode receives more emphasis than the others. For example, academia and writing teachers have historically favored the linguistic mode, often seen in the form of the written college essay. Yet, when you communicate using an essay, you are actually using three modes of communication: linguistic, spatial, and visual. The words represent the linguistic mode (the emphasized mode), the margins and spacing characterize the spatial, and the visual mode includes elements like font, font size, or the use of bold.

Combining each mode to create a clear communicative essay often involves the writing process (i.e. invention, drafting, and revision), and a thoughtful writer will also consider how the final product does or does not address an audience. The same process is used when creating a less traditional multimodal text. For instance, when creating a text emphasizing the aural mode (e.g. a podcast), you must consider your audience, purpose, and context while also organizing and arranging your ideas and content in a coherent and logical way. This process parallels the traditional writing process. Thus, while a multimodal text might be considered less "academic" by some students and/or instructors, understanding that all writing and all texts are also multimodal demonstrates that learning about multimodality and how to multimodally compose is just as important as learning how to write.

Why Is Multimodal Composing Important?

You might be wondering why you should multimodally compose in a college writing class. In this section, I provide some answers to this question. I explain how multimodal composing assignments help students practice digital literacy skills, offer an opportunity to transfer multimodal composing experiences from home to academic settings, and allow students to learn "real life" composing practices.

Multimodal Assignments Help You Learn Digital Literacy Skills

You have likely been taught that to succeed in the world, you need to become a literate citizen. The common understanding of "literate" or "literacy" is an ability to read and write alphabetic texts. While it is important to have these skills, this definition privileges words and language over the other modes of communication. It also does not allow for assignments that help you practice communicating using multiple literacies, modes of communication, and technologies in various and diverse writing situations.

The New London Group members were some of the first to argue that students should have opportunities to practice and learn multiple literacies in the classroom, while utilizing emerging technologies. This idea continues to be reflected in writing and literacy goals in many first year writing and writing across the curriculum courses. In fact, check out your syllabus; in many colleges and universities there is a goal related to "digital literacy." The 2000s saw the arrival of "digital literacy skills" added to many first year writing program's learning outcomes and include understanding how to react to different writing assignments that require composing practices beyond writing a college essay and learning how to use various technologies to appropriately distribute information. Multimodal assignments offer opportunities for instructors to help you learn these digital literacy skills.

Multimodal Assignments Allow You to Use What You Know

You are likely already sharing and creating multimodal texts online and communicating with a wide range of audiences through social media, which Ryan P. Shepherd argues, requires multimodality. However, in his 2018 study, Shepherd also points out that students struggle to perceive the connections between the digital and multimodal composing they do *outside of school* with the same types of assignments they are asked to complete *in school.* What does this mean? Well, it means you are probably already multimodally composing outside of school but you just didn't know it. Understanding that you are already composing multimodally in many digital spaces will help you transfer that knowledge and experience into your academic assignments. This understanding might also help alleviate any fears or anxiety you may have when confronted with an assignment that disrupts what you think writing should look like. You can take a deep breath and remember that practicing multimodal composing in school connects to the multimodal composing you likely practice outside of school.

Multimodal Assignments Offer Real Skills for the Workforce

Perhaps the most significant reason for learning how to compose multimodally is that it provides "real-life" skills that can help prepare students for careers. The United States continues to experience a "digital age" where employees are expected to have an understanding of how to use technology and communicate in various ways for various purposes. Takayoshi and Selfe argue that "[w]hatever profession students hope to enter in the 21st century . . . they can expect to read and be asked to help compose multimodal texts of various kinds . . ." (3). Additionally, professionals are also using the benefits of digital tools and multimodal composing to promote themselves, their interests, research, or all three. Learning how to create a multimodal text will prepare you for the workforce by allowing you to embrace the skills you already have and learn how to target specific audiences for specific reasons using various modes of communication.

How Do I Create a Multimodal Text?

Now that you know what a multimodal text is and why it is important to learn how to create them, it makes sense to discuss strategies for composing a multimodal text. As with writing, multimodal composing is a process and should not only emphasize the final result. Therefore, the first three strategies listed below are pre-drafting activities.

1. Determine your rhetorical situation.
2. Review and analyze other multimodal texts.
3. Gather content, media, and tools.
4. Cite and attribute information appropriately.
5. Begin drafting your text.

While I often ask my students to attend to each strategy in the order given, your process might change based on the assignment and/or instructor expectations.

Determine Your Rhetorical Situation

When brainstorming your rhetorical situation, you should consider the purpose of your text (*the message*), who you want to read and interact with your text (*the audience*), your relationship to the message and audience (*the author*), the type of text you want to create (*the genre*), and where you want to distribute it (*the medium*). Descriptions of each of the five components of the rhetorical situation are offered below.

The Message

The message relates to your purpose, and you might ask yourself, what am I trying to accomplish? You should try to make the message as clear and specific as possible. Let's say you want to create a website focused on donating to charity. An unclear message might be "getting more people in the United States to donate to charities." A clearer message is "convincing college freshmen at my university to donate to the ASPCA" because the audience and purpose are specific rather than broad.

The Audience

There are two types of audiences. An intended audience, who you target in your message, and an unintentional audience, who may stumble upon your text. When determining your message, you want to consider the beliefs, values, and demographics of your intended audience as well as the likelihood that unintentional audiences will interact with your text. Using the example above, college freshmen at your university are the intended audience, and teachers, parents, and/or students from other universities represent unintentional audience members. It might be helpful to approach audience using the concept of "discourse communities," or "a group of people, members of a community, who share a common interest and who use the same language, or discourse, as they talk and write about that interest" (National Council of Teachers of English). You can read more about discourse communities in Dan Melzer's essay, "You'll Never Write Alone Again: Understanding Discourse Communities" found in this volume of *Writing Spaces*.

The Author

You are the author and should consider your relationship to the message and audience. As an author, you bring explicit (obvious) and/or implicit (not obvious) biases to your message, so it is important to recognize how these might affect it and your audience. Also, you may be targeting an audience you are familiar with (perhaps you are also a college freshman) or not (perhaps you are a graduate student). It is important to think about how your familiarity might affect your message.

The Genre

Genre is a tricky term and can mean different things to different scholars, teachers, and students (Dirk 250). In the context of multimodal composing, genre refers to a type of text that has genre conventions, or audience expectations. For example, if I am creating a website (the genre), an audience would expect the following conventions: an easy-to-navigate toolbar, functional tabs, hyperlinks, and images. Yet, when thinking about genre, it is more useful to think specifically. If I am creating a website for horror film fans (the specific genre), then the audience would expect the following (more specific) genre conventions: references, images, and sounds associated with horror films, directors, actors, actresses, monsters, and villains. They would also expect color and font choices to align with the genre—it is likely that the color baby blue would not be well-received.

The Medium

While genre is the type of text you want to create, the medium refers to where you will distribute it. Classic media (plural for medium) includes distribution via radio, newspapers, magazines, and television; however, new media is defined by a text's online distribution. Importantly, medium refers to where you will distribute your text but not how. The how refers to the technology tools you'll use to create the text and possibly to distribute it. For example, to create a podcast, you might use your smartphone (a tool) to record, a free sound editor like Audacity (another tool) to edit it, and Soundcloud (a tool *and* the medium) to distribute it.

Review and Analyze Other Multimodal Texts

Now that you have brainstormed your rhetorical situation and determined the type of text you want to create, it is time to begin finding other texts representative of your topic and genre. In their textbook, *Writer/Designer: A Guide to Making Multimodal Projects*, Arola, Sheppard, and Ball argue that "[o]ne of the best ways to begin thinking about a multimodal project is to see *what* has already been said about a topic you are interested in . . . as well as *how* other authors have designed their texts on that topic . . . " (40). This is excellent advice. I suggest that you find at least one text you think is an exceptional example and one text you feel is lacking in some way. After you find these texts, you can conduct a brief analysis by responding to the following questions:

1. What is the author's message?
2. Who are they addressing? How can you tell?
3. What type of text did they create? What genre conventions do you see?
4. How was the text distributed? In what ways does it relate to the target audience?
5. What modes of communication are they using? Which are they emphasizing? Do these decisions support the message and/or appropriately target their audience?
6. What do you like about the multimodal text?
7. What, in your opinion, needs work?

If you answer these questions, you have given yourself important feedback to consider for your own work.

Gather Content, Media, and Tools

Once you have determined your rhetorical situation and examined other multimodal texts, you should begin gathering information and materials. I have categorized this process into three components: content, visual and aural materials, and technology tools.

Conduct Content Research

A multimodal text should include content (key pieces of information that support your message), which means you will need to conduct some research. The extent of the research depends on the type of assignment; some instructors might want your multimodal text to include scholarly research while others might not. Therefore, be sure to read the assignment closely and then conduct the necessary research. For example, my student created a website and videos discussing the similarities between American music and K-pop (see figure 6). Her content research includes a scholarly article from the journal *World Englishes* and a popular article from *Billboard.com*.

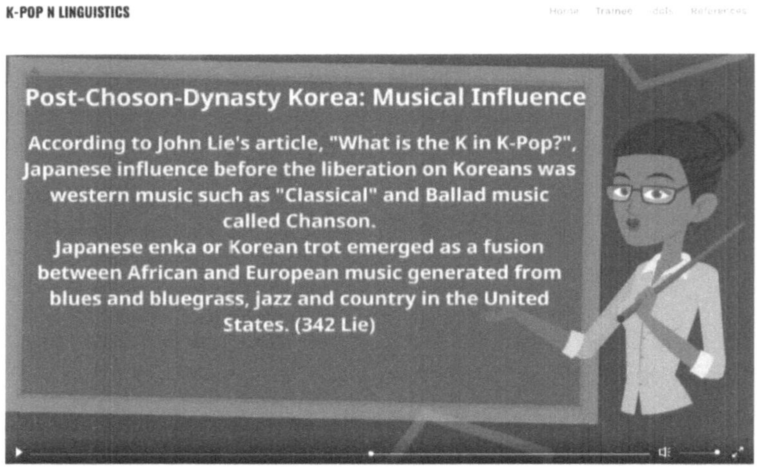

Figure 6. A screen shot of a student's video that illustrates her use of scholarly content. Video shows an animation of a teacher standing at a chalkboard. On the chalkboard, there is text explaining the musical influences on Post-Choson-Dynasty Korea. (Permission to use this image was obtained from the student).

Collect Visual and Aural Materials

In addition to textual information, you should also collect images, sounds, videos, animations, memes, etc. you want to include in your multimodal text. For instance, figure 6 demonstrates some of the pre-draft materials my student collected: openly licensed images of a teacher and chalkboard, a video they created using Animator, and K-Pop music to play on a loop.

Explore Openly Licensed Materials

When searching for visual and aural materials, you want to consider using openly licensed materials. According to *Yearofopen.org*, open licenses are "a set of conditions applied to an original work that grant permission for anyone to make use of that work as long as they follow the conditions of the license" ("What are Open Licenses"). A well-known and commonly used example of an open license are Creative Commons licenses, identified by CC. Creative Commons licenses provide the creator or author with a copyright, ensuring that they receive credit for their work, while also allowing "others to copy, distribute, and make uses of their work – at least non-commercially" ("About the Licenses"). Essentially, if a work has one of the four basic creative commons licenses (see figure 7), then a creator/author can use the licensed item in their own creative texts.

The most open license. An author can use it in any way as long as they provide attribution

Attribution
CC BY

Allows for any use but must attribute the author and the new work cannot be used for commercial gain.

Attribution-NonCommercial
CC BY-NC

An author must provide attribution and the new work must be shared with the same license as the original work

Attribution-ShareAlike
CC BY-SA

Allows for any use but must attribute the author and used in its original form with no changes to the original work.

Attribution-NoDerivs
CC BY-ND

Figure 7. The four basic Creative Commons licenses including explanations for each. (Image was created by the author using "About Licenses" by Creative Commons licensed under CC BY 4.0)

There are various websites such as CC Search, Free Music Archive (FMA), or Digital Public Library of America (DPLA) where you can find openly licensed work. You may also set filters on Flickr or Google Images to locate openly licensed work.

COLLECT AND EVALUATE TECHNOLOGY TOOLS

It is important to collect and evaluate the technology tools you need to create your multimodal text prior to drafting it. As stated previously, the technology tool helps you create the final text and might also help you distribute it. The easiest way to determine the technology tools that you need is to create a list of all of the features you want to include in your text. Once you create the list, research where to find the tools either online or at your university. Be aware that some tools may not be free (although they may come with a free trial period), but you can use software available on your computer or university computers such as iMovie or Windows Movie Maker. Or you can find freeware, software available for free online, such as Audacity (for sound editing), Canva (for infographic and/or image creation), or Blender (for video creation). Once you have created your list and found some tools, spend some time testing each one while keeping track of which is the most user-friendly and helps you achieve your composing goals.

Citing and Attributing Your Content

After researching content and collecting materials, think about how you will give rhetorically appropriate credit to authors or organizations whose work you have referenced or included. For instance, if you create a video, you should provide credits at the end rather than a Works Cited page, or if you design a website, you should include hyperlinks to outside sources rather than MLA in-text citations because this makes more sense, given the genre. For multimodal texts that rely on the aural mode (e.g. podcasts), you can use verbal attributions, or verbalize necessary information. When deciding what information is necessary, think about what you can include to help your audience locate your text, such as author, title, and website. For example, the phrase, "*According to Mandi Goodsett, in her PowerPoint 'Creative Commons Licenses' found on the library website, a student has control over their online presence*," offers the audience key information to help them find the source.

When citing openly licensed images, videos, sounds, animations, screenshots, etc., it is important to provide an attribution. According to the CC Wiki, an appropriate attribution should include the title, author, source (hyperlinked to the original website), and license (hyperlinked to the license information). Figure 8 represents example of an inappropriate attribution and figure 9 an ideal one.

Image taken from Goodsett PowerPoint. The attribution lacks a title, clear author, source link, and license

Figure 8. An example of an inappropriate attribution that lacks title, clear author, source link, and license. (Image was created by the author using "Creative Commons Licensing" by Mandi Goodsett licensed under CC BY 4.0)

Figure 9. An example of an ideal attribution, which includes a hyperlinked title for the image, a clear author name, and license information that is also hyperlinked. (Image was created by the author using "Creative Commons Licensing" by Mandi Goodsett licensed under CC BY 4.0)

BEGIN DRAFTING YOUR TEXT

Drafting your text should include outlining or mapping your project. This could take the form of writing all of the text you want to include in an outline if you have a word-heavy multimodal text like a website, drawing your design if you are creating a poster or commercial, or writing a script if you are creating a podcast or video. Of course, you can combine any of these outlining methods or come up with your own, but thinking about what you want to do before you do it will make your final text much stronger and coherent.

FINAL REMARKS AND FINDING MORE INFORMATION

The primary purpose of this chapter is to introduce you to multimodal composing and offer some strategies to help you create a multimodal text. Yet, just like with traditional writing, multimodal composing is a process, and while I provided three pre-drafting strategies, I did not offer much in the way of guidance for drafting your final product. Therefore, I would like to conclude by offering two excellent resources:

- Michael J. Klein and Kristi L. Shackelford's *Writing Spaces* volume 2 chapter, "Beyond Black on White: Document Design and Formatting in the Writing Classroom" discusses visual design, which can help you create your final text.
- Arola, Sheppard, and Ball's commercial textbook, *Writer/Designer: A Guide to Making Multimodal Projects* (first and second editions) offers detailed advice for making your multimodal text.

Works Cited

"About the Licenses." *Creativecommons.org*, https://creativecommons.org/licenses/. Accessed 29 May 2019.

Arola, Kristin L., Jennifer Sheppard, and Cheryl E. Ball. *Writer/Designer: A Guide to Making Multimodal Projects*. Bedford/St. Martin, 2014.

Ball, Cheryl E. and Colin Charlton. "All Writing is Multimodal." *Naming What we Know: Threshold Concepts of Writing Studies*, edited by Linda Adler-Kassner and Elizabeth Wardle, Utah State University Press 2015, pp. 42-43, https://ebookcentral-proquest-com.proxy-iup.klnpa.org/lib/indianauniv-ebooks/reader.action?docID=3442949&ppg=140.

CC Wiki. "Best practices for attribution." *Wiki.Creativecommons.org*, 9 July 2018, https://wiki.creativecommons.org/wiki/Best_practices_for_attribution. Accessed 29 May 2019.

Dirk, Kerry. "Navigating Genres." *Writing Spaces: Readings on Writing*, vol. 1, 2010, pp. 249-262, https://writingspaces.org/sites/default/files/dirk--navigating-genres.pdf. Accessed 28 May 2019.

Goodsett, Mandi. "Creative Commons Licensing." Cleveland State University, 2019, Google Slides, https://drive.google.com/file/d/1qZJVYF7S8TM_o1AkfTH2cYplvT2R83u9/view.

Klein, Michael J. and Kristi L. Shackelford. "Beyond Black on White: Document Design and Formatting in the Writing Classroom." *Writing Spaces: Readings on Writings*, vol. 2, 2011, pp. 333-349, https://writingspaces.org/sites/default/files/klein-and-shackelford--beyond-black-on-white.pdf. Accessed 28 May 2019.

Lauer, Claire. "Contending with Terms: 'Multimodal' and 'Multimedia' in the Academic and Public Spheres." *Multimodal Composition: A Critical Sourcebook*, edited by Claire Lutkewitte, Bedford/St.Martin's, 2014, pp. 22-41.

Melzer, Dan. "You'll Never Write Alone Again: Understanding Discourse Communities." *Writing Spaces: Readings on Writings*, vol. 3, 2019.

National Council of Teachers of English. "Discourse Community." *ncte.org*, 2012, http://www.ncte.org/library/NCTEFiles/Resources/Journals/CCC/0641-sep2012/CCC0641PosterDiscourse.pdf. Accessed 29 May 2019.

Shepherd, Ryan P. "Digital Writing, Multimodality, and Learning Transfer: Crafting Connections between Composition and Online Composing." *Computers and Composition*, vol. 28, 2018, pp. 103-114, https://doi.org/10.1016/j.compcom.2018.03.001.

Takayoshi, Pamela and Cynthia L. Selfe. "Thinking about Multimodality." *Multimodal Composition: Resources for Teachers*, edited by Cynthia L. Selfe, Hampton Press, Inc., 2007, pp. 1-12.

The New London Group. "A Pedagogy of Multiliteracies: Designing Social Futures." *Harvard Educational Review*, vol. 66, no.1, 1996, https://eclass.duth.gr/modules/document/file.php/ALEX03242/3.5.%20The%20New%20London%20Group.pdf. Accessed 28 May 2019.

"What are Open Licenses." *Yearofopen.org*, https://www.yearofopen.org/what-are-open-licenses/. Accessed 28 May 2019.

Teaching Resources for An Introduction to and Strategies for Multimodal Composing by Melanie Gagich

This chapter can be used by instructors who integrate various types of multimodal composing assignments into their curriculum because it offers students an introduction to multimodal composing and strategies to consider when asked to create a multimodal text. As a composition teacher who has taught multimodal projects since 2014, I have found that some students want to jump right in to creating their multimodal text while others do not know how to begin. To counteract this issue, I use a process-based strategy that includes discussion, practice, and production when teaching multimodal assignments. This chapter reflects that process in that it is split into two sections. The first section provides a conceptual overview of multimodality and its importance in college writing classrooms and the second half offers five strategies instructors can use to help students create a multimodal text.

This chapter can be read as a whole or broken into sections; however, I think it is most appropriate to read each major section separately. I find it is easier to begin a multimodal assignment by asking students to read the first section of the chapter to frame discussions of key terms associated with multimodal composing, the modes of communication, and the importance of multimodality. This section also provides examples (drawn from outside sources as well as from my students' work), which I use as a basis for activities that ask students to respond to the chapter examples and then find their own. I have provided discussion questions and in-class activities that I have used to help students understand the concept of multimodality.

I assign the second section of the chapter after the initial introduction to key terms and multimodality. The second section includes three pre-drafting and two drafting strategies I have used successfully in my courses. The length of the project affects the way I utilize the second section of the chapter. For example, when I assign a semester-long multimodal project in an upper-level composition course, students are given a mini-project for each of the pre-drafting phases that helps them create a culminating multimodal text. In my first-year writing courses, I assign a four-week multimodal project, and I simply ask students to read the second half of the chapter and complete complementary in-class activities.

However, I can envision instances where the strategies could be addressed individually and/or rearranged. The second half of the chapter is meant to help students begin constructing a multimodal text, and provides a rough template for setting up a multimodal project unit for the instructor. By no means am I suggesting that the considerations listed here are inclusive of all possible ways of integrating a multimodal project; instead, I wanted to share these best practices with interested instructors to decrease the workload of creating a new project curriculum from scratch.

Discussion Questions

1. What does it mean to compose multimodally?
2. The chapter lists three reasons supporting the inclusion of multimodal composing assignments in writing classes; what are they? Why else might learning how to compose a multimodal text be important?
3. How is citing and attributing work in a multimodal text similar to and different from citing in a traditional MLA essay?

In-Class Activities

1. The chapter discusses and provides examples for the five modes of communication; find at least one example of each mode, different from those described in the chapter. Write one to two sentences explaining how it is representative of that mode.
2. What are openly licensed sources? Find at least three examples of an openly licensed source, describe the type of license they hold, and create an ideal attribution for each.
3. Find a multimodal text that relates to your topic or a topic of interest. Practice analyzing it using the questions from the "Review and Analyze other Multimodal Texts" sub-section. How can you use this analysis to help you create your own multimodal text?
4. Find a multimodal text and a traditional, written text that discusses your topic or a topic of interest. Does the presentation of information affect your understanding of each text? In what ways?

6 Grammar, Rhetoric, and Style

Craig Hulst

Overview

This chapter focuses on grammar, specifically on understanding that grammar is much more than just the rules that we have been taught. Rather, grammar can be used rhetorically—with an understanding of the writing situation and making appropriate choices regarding the structure of the sentences, the use of punctuation, using active or passive voice, etc. In other words, this chapter focuses on using grammar to influence a piece of writing's style, rather than focusing on the correctness of the grammar. Readers are encouraged to look at the writing that they see in their casual or research reading and evaluate the grammar of those pieces to gain a better understanding of how they can control their own use of grammar.

Grammar.[1] The mere word makes adults weep, children run and hide, and dogs howl.* All right, perhaps I am exaggerating just a bit; not all of us hate grammar. There are even people who actually like grammar. However, the general aversion to the word "grammar" is such that the word is hardly ever used in polite company. And, if your composition professor is anything like me, she or he tries to avoid the word in your class.

Yet grammar should not be so disrespected. Believe it or not, most people like grammar until their junior high school English teacher gets ahold of them and presents grammar as a set of rules, a set of "Thou shalt not" commandments that you must abide by or be doomed to wander in the darkness of a poor grade. Max Morenberg, author of the book *Doing Grammar*, writes:

---

* This work is licensed under the Creative Commons Attribution-NonCommercial-NoDerivatives 4.0 International License (CC BY-NC-ND 4.0) and are subject to the Writing Spaces Terms of Use. To view a copy of this license, visit http://creativecommons.org/licenses/by-nc-nd/4.0/, email info@creativecommons.org, or send a letter to Creative Commons, PO Box 1866, Mountain View, CA 94042, USA. To view the Writing Spaces Terms of Use, visit http://writingspaces.org/terms-of-use.

> We are born to love language and everything associated with it—rhythm, rhyme, word meanings, grammar. If you want to make a three-year-old child roll on the floor laughing, just tell her a riddle, or alliterative words, or read her Dr. Seuss's lilting rhythms and rhymes about cats in hats or elephants who are 'faithful, one hundred percent' or Sam I Am eating green eggs and ham on a boat with a goat. Listen to a child in a crib entertaining himself by repeating sounds and syllables, playing with language. Think about the games you played in kindergarten by creating strange words like Mary Poppins' supercalifragilisticexpialodotious. Keep a ten-year old entertained on a car trip by producing odd sentences in a 'Mad Libs' game. Then ask an eighth grader what subject she hates most. The answer invariably will be grammar. We're born to love grammar. We're taught to hate it. (vii-viii)

When young and learning how to use language, we learn grammar through trial and error. When my daughters were around two years old, they (constantly) wanted me to pick them up. They would come up to me, hold up their arms, and I would ask them, "Do you want me to hold you?" Eventually, they would come up to me, hold up their arms, and say, "hold you." They learned the construction "hold you" to mean "hold me." I would correct them and explain to them "if you want me to pick you up, you say 'hold me.'" Before too long they caught on and started saying "hold me" when they wanted me to pick them up. They learned by mirroring my speech and by receiving feedback on their grammar. As we grow older, we still learn through trial and error, but we also learn the rules. Now, instead of a parent's gentle correction, we are informed of our errors through the fiery correction of a teacher's red pen.

Grammar, the way that it is typically taught, is a collection of rules that we are supposed to follow, and it is these rules that most of us have issues with. After all, we know how to speak; we form words and sentences intuitively, and people understand our meaning. So, who are these rule-mongering grammarians that think that they can tell us that we are doing it wrong? Or who force us, as my middle school English teacher did, to endlessly diagram sentence after sentence? Why do they take something that we love as children and warp it to the point that we can't stand it?

Grammar doesn't have to be this way. It shouldn't be this way. We shouldn't need someone to tell us that we are wrong, and then to make us memorize a bunch of rules in order to speak or write. What grammar should be is a tool to help us better communicate with our audience—a tool that we are controlling, rather than one that controls us. Grammar should be a tool that we use to fit our language to our purpose and our audience.

Grammar and Its Rhetorical Use

The rules are there for a reason. Grammar rules are concerned with correctness—to make sure that we are following the accepted guidelines of the language. However, grammar isn't all about rules. Instead, grammar is about making meaning. People understand us because we are using grammar—we are arranging our words in a certain order, and because of that, our audience understands us. For example, if I said, "store went to Jim the," you'd probably ask, "What?" But if I used the same words and arranged the words according to the grammar that I absorbed at a young age, I would say, "Jim went to the store." By arranging the words according to what those listening to me expect from my grammar, my audience would know exactly what I meant. And this awareness of what the audience needs is the heart of what I am talking about—that grammar has a *rhetorical* use.

Grammar simply means "a system that puts words together into meaningful units" (Morenberg 4). We've already seen how that works in the earlier example of "Jim went to the store." As we create lengthier and more complex sentences, we incorporate punctuation such as commas and semicolons, consider pronoun/antecedent connections, carefully think about verb shifts and a host of other issues that can affect the meaning of our words. This is what most people think of when they hear the word grammar. However, this doesn't have to be that big of a concern, as grammar is best learned by using the language, rather than through systematic study of the rules. In fact, I have had many older, so-called non-traditional students in my composition classes throughout the years, and they are generally more adept at grammar usage than my "traditional" eighteen to twenty-year-old students. This is not because they have studied the rules of grammar more thoroughly; most of my older students confess that they haven't thought about grammar for many years. This is simply because they have used the language, and have experience using it in many different contexts, for a greater length of time.

Rhetoric is a word that most of us have heard, but we may not really understand what it means. It is a word that is often thrown around negatively, and often in political discussions, such as, "Well, the president may think that way, but I'm not falling for his rhetoric." But the term really shouldn't have such a negative connotation. Simply defined, rhetoric is "a way of using language for a specific purpose." The *rhetorical situation* of a piece of writing is everything surrounding it—who the audience is, the purpose for writing it, the genre of the writing, etc. Knowing this helps us know how to use language to accomplish the purpose of the writing, and grammar is part of that use of language. English professor Laura R. Micciche expands on the rhetorical role of grammar:

> The grammatical choices we make—including pronoun use, active or passive verb construction, and sentence construction—represent relations between writers and the world they live in. Word choice and sentence structure are an expression of the way we attend to the words of others, the way we position ourselves in relation to others. (719)

When we write, we can carefully choose the grammar that we use to make our writing effective at conveying our meaning, but also give the audience a sense of our own personality. This brings us to a third word that needs to be defined: *Style*.

Grammar and Style

Style is perhaps the most visual aspect of rhetoric—we see authors' style in their writing. Style refers to the choices that an author makes—choices about punctuation, word usage, and grammar—and those choices are influenced by the rhetorical situation that the author finds herself in. For example, consider the following sentences:

- Katelyn was concerned that Chloe worked late every night.
- It concerned Katelyn that every night Chloe worked late.
- Chloe worked late every night, and Katelyn was concerned.
- Every night Chloe worked late, and that concerned Katelyn.

Each of these sentences say the same thing, and the grammar is "correct" in each, but the sentence an author chooses depends on the style she wishes to use. The first sentence is the most straightforward, but the last two put the emphasis on Chloe rather than on Katelyn, which might be what the author wants to do. Sometimes the style within a specific rhetorical situation is prescribed for us; for example, we might be told that we cannot use "I" in a paper. Sometimes the style is expected, but we aren't necessarily told the rhetorical situation's rules; we might be expected to use the active voice rather than the passive voice in our papers. And sometimes the situation is wide open, allowing us to make the grammatical style choices we like.

Also wrapped up in this issue of style is the concept of standard and preferred usage. *Usage* is simply the way we expect words to be used—and this doesn't always follow the rules. For example, a famous line from the original *Star Trek* series tells us that the Enterprise's mission is "to boldly go where no man has gone before." This seems right—but there is a split infinitive in the phrase (no need to worry about what a split infinitive is right now). To abide by the rule, the line should say, "to go boldly where no man has gone before." But that doesn't sound as right to most of us, so a decision was made to break the rule and write the line according to the common usage of adding an adverb before the verb.

What usage is preferred is also dependent on the rhetorical situation of the text. As an example of the differences between standard and preferred usage, consider contractions. Most of the time when we speak, and often in informal writing, it is perfectly fine to use contractions like "can't," "isn't," or "aren't;" contractions are standard usage. You may have been told in your composition class that using contractions is okay in your papers, but using contractions is not preferred in many rhetorical situations, as in a formally written research paper. We use the words "I" and "you" all the time when we speak, but we will find many writing situations where they aren't acceptable (i.e. preferred). Knowing what usage is preferred takes a little insight into the rhetorical situation—you can read examples of the type of writing that you are asked to do, you can question friends who have already taken the course, you can seek advice from books or the internet, or you can ask your instructor. Since grammar, style, and usage are so closely related, and quite possibly they have already been introduced to you as the same thing, throughout this essay I will often refer to these types of style choices as grammar choices.

All Together Now

When we write, we are entering into a conversation with our reader, and the grammatical choices that we consciously make can show our readers that we understand what they want from us, and that we are giving them what they expect. In your academic writing, the rhetorical situation demands that you make grammar choices that are appropriate for college-level writers. Unfortunately, these grammar choices are not static; they will change—perhaps only slightly, perhaps greatly—as your writing situation changes, as you write for different teachers, courses, or disciplines. In your other writing, the rhetorical situation may call for an entirely different set of grammar choices.

Here's an example of how the rhetorical situation affects grammar usage. You need to express an idea concerning the need to recycle. In the first rhetorical situation, you are speaking to your friends, people that you have known since you were five years old. In such a situation, it might be acceptable for you to say, "It ain't rocket science, bonehead. Recycle that junk and save the Earth." If you're speaking to your mother, you might say, "Mom, that can go in the recycling bin instead. Let's save the planet." If you are writing about this for an academic audience, you might instead say, "We must always consider the consequences of our actions. Throwing recyclable materials in the trash results in overflowing landfills, land and water pollution, and an increased strain on raw materials. However, recycling glass, metal, and paper reduces our consumption of these materials as well as lowers the fossil fuel energy needed to create new products." The example should not suggest that longer sentences are more correct, although the academic audience example is considerably longer than the other two. Hopefully, if I have done it right, the academic audience example is longer simply because I am proving my point, not because I'm trying to sound smart by using more words. But the grammar has also changed. In the first example, I used "ain't," which is not considered grammatically correct for most academic audiences, but the use of which is quite common in many varieties of spoken English. In the second example I used the contraction "can't," which, again, in many academic writing situations would be frowned upon. In the final example, I have attempted to use "standard" grammar, the grammar that the academic rules say I should use, as I know that that particular audience would expect me to do so.

In many academic writing situations, the work is assessed, in part, on how well the writer adheres to the rules. If I used the style and grammar of the first example in a paper for my Environmental Science class, you can imagine what could happen. Writing an academic paper as if I was talking to my friends would probably negatively affect my grade. However, the poor grade wouldn't mean, "your grammar is wrong," even if my instructor phrased it that way. Instead, what the grade would mean is that I did not use the appropriate grammar required for the rhetorical situation.

Using Grammar Rhetorically for Style

Grammarian and textbook author Martha Kolln asks us to look at sentences as a series of slots into which we place words (5). We know what to put into certain slots; for example, in the "subject" slot we know we need a noun or a pronoun, and in the "verb" slot we need, well, a verb. Knowing just these two slots, I can make a good sentence: "I laughed." As sentences get more and more sophisticated, more slots become available. For example, adding an adverb slot, I can create the following sentence: "I laughed loudly." This is a basic element of the rules—the rules tell us what we are allowed to put into the slots.

So then, how do we move past the rules? How does a writer use grammar rhetorically? First and foremost, you use grammar this way by being conscious of the choices that you are making. Remember, when you write, you aren't simply putting words on paper; you are constructing a conversation with a reader. You make conscious choices about your topic, your title, and your word choice, as well as many other choices, in order to carry on that conversation—grammar is just part of the many choices that you can use to your advantage when you are using language for your specific purpose. It might help you to see how this is done by looking at works that have been written for a variety of audiences and trying to figure out why the authors made the grammatical choices that they did.

Throughout the rest of this essay, I will present several examples of writing, and I will look at what each author has chosen to put into their sentence slots and why they made those choices. The first example is a paragraph from the manual for the video game *Fallout 3*:

> Nuclear war. The very words conjure images of mushroom clouds, gas masks, and bewildered children ducking and covering under their school desks. But it's the aftermath of such a conflict that truly captures our imagination, in large part because there's no real-world equivalent we can relate to. Mankind may have witnessed the horror of the atomic bomb, but thankfully we've somehow succeeded in not blowing up the entire planet. At least, not yet. (*Vault Dweller's Survival Guide* 3)

This paragraph violates many of the rules that I learned as a developing writer. For example, I see the contractions *it's*, *there's*, and *we've*, and a conjunction, *but*, starts a sentence. I see the preposition *to* ending a sentence—a definite no-no, if I remember my grammar rules. Also, as I write this on my computer, my word processor is very kindly informing me that there are two fragments in this paragraph. I believe that Ms. Herrema, my eighth grade English teacher, would cringe if she read this paragraph in a student paper. Yet I think it unlikely that you noticed all of these "errors" in the paragraph as you read it. Why didn't you? Is it because you are ignorant of the rules of grammar? Absolutely not! Assuming that you didn't notice them, you didn't notice them because taken all together, the paragraph flowed well. The fragment sentence, *Nuclear war,* didn't bother you—in fact, it probably grabbed your attention. The contractions didn't bother you because it sounded like someone was speaking to you. And they were.

The intended audience of the writer is those who would buy and play video games. (That might include you—it does include me.) As such, the author knowledgeably chose the language, the grammar, of the game manual in order to maintain the interest of the audience. We speak with contractions; the author uses contractions. We speak in fragments; the author uses them. Notice that the author is using the fragments ominously. He (or she, but probably they—much professional writing is team written) begins with *Nuclear war.* Culturally, we have, for the past seventy years or so, lived with the knowledge that a nuclear war could happen. Those two words conjure up such dark and depressing images that all the author needs to do is say them, and we're hooked. Likewise, the last sentence of the paragraph is also a fragment, ominous, and attention grabbing: *At least, not yet.* We have dodged this atomic bullet until now, but it could still happen—and that is what the author wishes to leave us with.

Let's look at how the commas are used in this paragraph. The first commas that we see are in the list: *mushroom clouds, gas masks, and bewildered children.* Why does the author put those commas there? Is it because the rules tell him to? Yes—and no. Sure, the rules tell us to put those commas in there, but if we're relying on the rhetorical use of grammar, we'll also use them in exactly the same way. A comma indicates a pause in a sentence, a pause that the audience needs in order to get the meaning the author intends to give them. Read that sentence out loud without the commas: *The very words conjure images of mushroom clouds gas masks and bewildered children ducking and covering under their school desks.* Without the commas, it sounds weird. Your audience might even see this as five-item list of mushroom, clouds, gas, masks, and bewildered children, rather than the three-item list that it is. If the author's meaning is for the audience to see mushroom clouds and gas masks and bewildered children, regardless of the rules, he would add a comma to make them pause, just a bit, at certain points.

Let's move from the popular to the academic in this next example:

> The typewriter is effectively a lost technology, occupying a strange, interstitial space in the broader field of media history, a fulcrum between the movable type of modern print culture and the malleable digital information of postmodern electronic culture. I argue that consideration of the typewriter as a writing system thus pro-

vides critical purchase on this field precisely to the extent that the machine itself is ephemeral and ultimately obsolete. (Benzon 93)

Did you get all that? You probably noticed the difference in vocabulary between this paragraph and the passage from game manual. This author is definitely writing for a different audience; in this case, he is writing for English scholars and educators. If we look at the first sentence as a series of slots, we see *typewriter* in the subject slot, *is* in the verb slot, and *technology* in the object slot. But we also see *effectively* and *lost* in the sentence, occupying two optional slots. *Lost* is positioned in an adjective slot and describes *technology*. What kind of technology? *Lost* technology. *Effectively* is positioned in an adverb slot, and as such it modifies the verb. *Is* what? Is *effectively*. We could have eliminated these two modifiers and the sentence would have made sense. But Benzon, the author, did not want to say that "The typewriter is a technology." He wanted to say that it was *effectively* a *lost* technology. Typewriters still exist, and people still use them, although they are *effectively a lost technology*.

Notice, too, that there are other optional slots that were not filled. *Typewriter*, as a noun, has an optional adjective slot, too. But instead of describing the typewriters, Benzon chooses not to fill in that slot. Doing so might restrict the noun—adding an adjective to describe what type of typewriters are lost technology could limit the meaning. Adding an adjective like *red*, *old*, or *dusty* would say that typewriters that are blue, new, or clean are not lost technology.

Benzon also chooses to use the grammatical device of parallelism in the phrase, "a fulcrum between the movable type of modern print culture and the malleable digital information of postmodern electronic culture." *Movable type* runs parallel to *malleable digital information*. In both situations, we see nouns (*type* and *information*) preceded by filled adjective slots. *Movable* and *malleable* even sound similar. Benzon opted to fill in another adjective slot before *information* and told us that it was *digital* information but decided not to do so before *type*. This is acceptable, of course, because *type* does not need any additional description, but we certainly need to know what sort of information is malleable.

Finally, we see in this example that Benzon uses *I*. This convention is generally acceptable in the discipline of the humanities, and knowing that his audience would accept this, Benzon has decided to use *I*. He also uses the active voice, writing, "I argue that consideration of the typewriter as a writing system…" The author, *I*, is doing something, arguing. (In this case, my middle school English teacher's advice to write in the active voice has been justified.) Had I not told you that both the use of *I* and the active voice were acceptable in the humanities, analyzing the previous paragraph would have shown that this was true.

And now let's try one more, this time from an academic article from the sciences:

> Animals were randomly assigned to three treatment groups with five pigs per group in a completely randomized design. All pigs were fed the basal diet during the initial 7 day period. Pigs were then fed treatment diets during the next three 7 day periods and all pigs received the basal diet during the final two 7 day periods. (Stewart et al. 169)

This excerpt comes from an article in the *American Journal of Animal and Veterinary Sciences*, so who do you think is the intended audience? If you said, "circus clowns," you might want to try again.

Obviously, we see vocabulary that is intended for veterinarians or students of veterinary medicine. The main reason that I have offered this passage to you, aside from the fact that I enjoy torturing people with language, is that we can see two differences between this piece of academic writing and the previous piece. The first is that there is no use of *I*. Why didn't the authors say, "*We fed* the pigs the basal diet during the initial 7 day period?" The reason is that, unlike in the humanities disciplines, the use of the personal pronoun is not expected by a science audience. Using it would be counter to the expectations of the audience, so it isn't used. (Score one for the middle school English teacher who told me not to use *I*.)

The second difference from the Benzon passage is that the subjects of the sentences aren't doing anything; this passage is written in the passive voice. Whereas Benzon could say, "I argue," which showed the active subject *I* doing something (arguing), in this piece, the pigs are passive receptors of the food. They sit there; food is given to them. If this was recast in active voice, we might end up with, "All pigs *ate* the basal diet during the initial 7 day period." Unlike the humanities disciplines, the sciences have a tendency to prefer the passive voice. Again, if I hadn't just told you these two conventions of science writing, had you rhetorically analyzed the piece, analyzed its audience, purpose, and grammar, you would have seen that these conventions exist.

If you'd like a fourth example, consider this essay that you are reading. Ask yourself why I made the grammatical choices that I did. I use "you," I use contractions, I tend to use the active voice. There a few fragment sentences in here—the first sentence of the essay is a fragment. Why would I write with these rule violations?

Did you notice the "errors" I listed above as you read through the paper? I am guessing that you did not, or at least you did not catch all of them. If I have done my job right, I have successfully entered into a conversation with you—a first year writing student—and spoken to you using a grammar that is comfortable and appropriate for you. How did I do?

With these four examples, I've only given you a taste of how looking at grammar choices rhetorically can help you understand an author's intended audience, that audience's expectations, and how the author, by choosing his or her grammar to reflect those needs, attempted to enter into a relationship with the audience. You could spend quite a bit of time on any of those examples and pull even more insights from the grammar that the authors use, but given the scope of this essay, I believe that I can now safely let you go, believing that you now have a solid understanding of how writers—and that includes you—make careful choices with their grammar and use it as a tool to more effectively communicate with their intended audience.

Note

1. Throughout this essay, I will use some simple grammar terms such as noun, pronoun, adjective, adverb, and so on. I am, perhaps wrongly, assuming that you will understand these terms. If I have erred in my assumption, please accept my apologies. There are many ways to discover the meanings of these terms, the first of which is your instructor. Other resources include handbooks, internet sources, and your friends.

Works Cited

Benzon, Paul. "Lost in Transcription: Postwar Typewriting Culture, Andy Warhol's Bad Book, and the Standardization of Error." *PMLA*, vol. 125, no. 1, 2010, pp. 92–106. *JSTOR,* www.jstor.org/stable/25614438.

Kolln, Martha. *Rhetorical Grammar.* Longman, 2003.

Micciche, Laura R. "Making a Case for Rhetorical Grammar." *College Composition and Communication*, vol. 55, no. 4, Jun.2004, pp. 716-737. *ProQuest,* http://search.proquest.com.ezproxy.gvsu.edu/docview/62073590?accountid=39473.

Morenberg, Max. *Doing Grammar.* Oxford UP, 1997.

Stewart, L. L., Beob G. Kim, B. R. Gramm, R. D. Nimmo, and H. H. Stein. "Effects of Dietary Carbadox on Apparent Ileal Digestibility of Amino Acids in Weanling Pigs." *American Journal of Animal and Veterinary Sciences*, vol. 5 no. 3, 2010, pp. 168-174. https://nutrition.ansci.illinois.edu/sites/default/files/AmJAnimVetSci5.168-174.pdf

Vault Dweller's Survival Guide. Bethesda Softworks. 2008.

Teacher Resources for Grammar, Rhetoric, and Style by Craig Hulst

Overview and Teaching Strategies

When I ask my students about the weaknesses of their own writing, the vast majority state that grammar is an issue for them. Usually what they mean is that they do not remember the rules that they were taught and believe that without the rules, their writing must be weak. This essay is designed to be used to help students understand that grammar is more than just rules. Grammar can be used as a tool to influence the style of the piece, and students already implicitly have some understanding of how to use it that way.

This essay would best be used when a teacher is talking about either grammar or style. When talking about grammar, it could be linked with a discussion of why first year writing courses do not typically spend much time on the rules of grammar. When discussing style, it can be used in conjunction with understanding how the rhetorical situation influences style, and how grammar is one element of choosing an appropriate voice and style for that particular situation. It might be particularly useful when discussing revising, rather than drafting.

Questions

1. Before reading this piece, what was your reaction to hearing the word grammar? Did you like studying grammar? Did you hate it? After reading this piece, has your impression of the word changed at all?
2. Has grammar only been presented to you as a set of rules before? Why do you think it was taught that way?
3. In the personal example in the essay, the author wrote about his daughters learning to say "hold me" instead of "hold you" at two years old, but grammar is constantly developing as we are constantly developing our language. Do you remember any of the moments when you realized that the way that you used the language needed to be adjusted, or when you discovered that your grammar usage was not correct? What was it?
4. For the most part, it is less important that you understand all of the rules or grammatical terms than it is that you can recognize when

something doesn't sound right. However, this "sounds right" part of grammar can trip you up if you are trying to complete grammar exercises, as that usually means that you are responding to usage (the way most people seem to be using the grammar) instead of correctness (following the rules). Usage and correctness are often the same, but many times they are not. Are there any times that you can remember where you were corrected for using grammar according to usage instead of correctness? Why do you think that the usage is different from the rule? (Note to teacher: this question might best be used in conjunction with a grammar exercise to illustrate the difference of usage and correctness, possibly followed with a discussion of the style benefits of either).

5. Choose a passage from an essay that you have written. What grammatical choices did you make? What choices (word choice, the choice to fill in a slot or not, parallel structure, etc.) did you make? Which choices did you choose not to make? Should/can you continue to make choices that will give your audience what they expect to see?

ACTIVITIES

RHETORICAL GRAMMAR ANALYSIS

There are essays in *Writing Spaces* that talk about reading rhetorically (See Mike Bunn's and/or Karen Rosenberg's essays, for example). Combining this essay with one of those, ask students to look specifically at the grammar of a chosen piece of writing. Starting simply, ask them to look at the use of pronouns or contractions. What does the way that those parts of speech are used (or not used) say about the author's choices, about the intended audience? Move on to modifiers and look at the use of adjectives and adverbs. Are they widely used or are they sparse? Are there two or three modifiers for a noun or one? What do those decisions say about the rhetorical situation? Choose any other element of grammar and continue the analysis.

REVISING GRAMMAR FOR STYLE

Have students take a paper that they are revising and have them specifically look at their grammar. Ask them to identify their audience and the expectations of their writing. If they have already tried their hands at the *Rhetorical Grammar Analysis* activity, they might be able to apply what they have learned about how the author used grammar to create an appropriate style to their own writing. Otherwise, ask them about the level of formality that is expected in their writing and whether or not their use of grammar (pronoun usage, including gender-specific pronouns; contractions; complexity of sentence construction; etc.) supports that. Students might choose specific sentences and rewrite them (making active voice passive, adding modifiers, changing the verb tense, etc.) to see how the style of the sentence can be altered by grammatical choices.

7 Understanding Discourse Communities

Dan Melzer

Overview

This chapter uses John Swales' definition of *discourse community* to explain to students why this concept is important for college writing and beyond. The chapter explains how genres operate within discourse communities, why different discourse communities have different expectations for writing, and how to understand what qualifies as a discourse community. The article relates the concept of discourse community to a personal example from the author (an acoustic guitar jam group) and an example of the academic discipline of history. The article takes a critical stance regarding the concept of discourse community, discussing both the benefits and constraints of communicating within discourse communities. The article concludes with writerly questions students can ask themselves as they enter new discourse communities in order to be more effective communicators.

Last year, I decided that if I was ever going to achieve my lifelong fantasy of being the first college writing teacher to transform into an international rock star, I should probably graduate from playing the video game *Guitar Hero* to actually learning to play guitar.* I bought an acoustic guitar and started watching every beginning guitar instructional video on YouTube. At first, the vocabulary the online guitar teachers used was like a foreign language to me—terms like major and minor chords, open G tuning, and circle of fifths. I was overwhelmed by how complicated it all was, and the fingertips on my left hand felt like they were going to fall off from pressing on the steel strings on the neck of my guitar to form

---

* This work is licensed under the Creative Commons Attribution-NonCommercial-NoDerivatives 4.0 International License (CC BY-NC-ND 4.0) and are subject to the Writing Spaces Terms of Use. To view a copy of this license, visit http://creativecommons.org/licenses/by-nc-nd/4.0/, email info@creativecommons.org, or send a letter to Creative Commons, PO Box 1866, Mountain View, CA 94042, USA. To view the Writing Spaces Terms of Use, visit http://writingspaces.org/terms-of-use.

chords. I felt like I was making incredibly slow progress, and at the rate I was going, I wouldn't be a guitar god until I was 87. I was also getting tired of playing alone in my living room. I wanted to find a community of people who shared my goal of learning songs and playing guitar together for fun.

I needed a way to find other beginning and intermediate guitar players, and I decided to try a social media website called "Meetup.com." It only took a few clicks to find the right community for me—an "acoustic jam" group that welcomed beginners and met once a month at a music store near my city of Sacramento, California. On the Meetup.com site, it said that everyone who showed up for the jam should bring a few songs to share, but I wasn't sure what kind of music they played, so I just showed up at the next meet-up with my guitar and the basic look you need to become a guitar legend: two days of facial hair stubble, black t-shirt, ripped jeans, and a gravelly voice (luckily my throat was sore from shouting the lyrics to the Twenty One Pilots song "Heathens" while playing guitar in my living room the night before).

The first time I played with the group, I felt more like a junior high school band camp dropout then the next Jimi Hendrix. I had trouble keeping up with the chord changes, and I didn't know any scales (groups of related notes in the same key that work well together) to solo on lead guitar when it was my turn. I had trouble figuring out the patterns for my strumming hand since no one took the time to explain them before we started playing a new song. The group had some beginners, but I was the least experienced player.

It took a few more meet-ups, but pretty soon I figured out how to fit into the group. I learned that they played all kinds of songs, from country to blues to folk to rock music. I learned that they chose songs with simple chords so beginners like me could play along. I learned that they brought print copies of the chords and lyrics of songs to share, and if there were any difficult chords in a song, they included a visual of the chord shape in the handout of chords and lyrics. I started to learn the musician's vocabulary I needed to be familiar with to function in the group, like *beats per measure* and *octaves* and the *minor pentatonic scale*. I learned that if I was having trouble figuring out the chord changes, I could watch the better guitarists and copy what they were doing. I also got good advice from experienced players, like soaking your fingers in rubbing alcohol every day for ninety seconds to toughen them up so the steel strings wouldn't hurt as much. I even realized that although I was an inexperienced player, I could contribute to the community by bringing in new songs they hadn't played before.

Okay, at this point you may be saying to yourself that all of this will make a great biographical movie someday when I become a rock icon (or maybe not), but what does it have to do with becoming a better writer?

You can write in a journal alone in your room, just like you can play guitar just for yourself alone in your room. But most writers, like most musicians, learn their craft from studying experts and becoming part of a community. And most writers, like most musicians, want to be a part of community and communicate with other people who share their goals and interests. Writing teachers and scholars have come up with the concept of "discourse community" to describe a community of people who share the same goals, the same methods of communicating, the same genres, and the same lexis (specialized language).

What Exactly Is a Discourse Community?

John Swales, a scholar in linguistics, says that discourse communities have the following features (which I'm paraphrasing):

1. A broadly agreed upon set of common public goals
2. Mechanisms of intercommunication among members
3. Use of these communication mechanisms to provide information and feedback
4. One or more genres that help further the goals of the discourse community
5. A specific lexis (specialized language)
6. A threshold level of expert members (24-26)

I'll use my example of the monthly guitar jam group I joined to explain these six aspects of a discourse community.

A broadly Agreed Set of Common Public Goals

The guitar jam group had shared goals that we all agreed on. In the Meetup.com description of the site, the organizer of the group emphasized that these monthly gatherings were for having fun, enjoying the music, and learning new songs. "Guitar players" or "people who like music" or even "guitarists in Sacramento, California" are not discourse communities. They don't share the same goals, and they don't all interact with each other to meet the same goals.

Mechanisms of Intercommunication among Members

The guitar jam group communicated primarily through the Meetup.com site. This is how we recruited new members, shared information about when and where we were playing, and communicated with each other outside of the night of the guitar jam. "People who use Meetup.com" are not a discourse community, because even though they're using the same method of communication, they don't all share the same goals and they don't all regularly interact with each other. But a Meetup.com group like the Sacramento acoustic guitar jam focused on a specific topic with shared goals and a community of members who frequently interact can be considered a discourse community based on Swales' definition.

Use of These Communication Mechanisms to Provide Information and Feedback

Once I found the guitar jam group on Meetup.com, I wanted information about topics like what skill levels could participate, what kind of music they played, and where and when they met. Once I was at my first guitar jam, the primary information I needed was the chords and lyrics of each song, so the handouts with chords and lyrics were a key means of providing critical information to community members. Communication mechanisms in discourse communities can be emails, text messages, social media tools, print texts, memes, oral presentations, and so on. One reason that Swales uses the term "discourse" instead of "writing" is that the term "discourse" can mean any type of communication, from talking to writing to music to images to multimedia.

One or More Genres That Help Further the Goals of the Discourse Community

One of the most common ways discourse communities share information and meet their goals is through genres. To help explain the concept of genre, I'll use music since I've been talking about playing guitar and music is probably an example you can relate to. Obviously there are many types of music, from rap to country to reggae to heavy metal. Each of these types of music is considered a genre, in part because the music has shared features, from the style of the music to the subject of the lyrics to the lexis. For example, most rap has a steady bass beat, most rappers use spoken word rather singing, and rap lyrics usually draw on a lexis associated with young people. But a genre is much more than a set of features. Genres arise out of social purposes, and they're a form of social action within discourse communities. The rap battles of today have historical roots in African oral contests, and modern rap music can only be understood in the context of hip hop culture, which includes break dancing and street art. Rap also has social purposes, including resisting social oppression and telling the truth about social conditions that aren't always reported on by news outlets. Like all genres, rap is not just a formula but a tool for social action.

The guitar jam group used two primary genres to meet the goals of the community. The Meetup.com site was one important genre that was critical in the formation of the group and to help it recruit new members. It was also the genre that delivered information to the members about what the community was about and where and when the community would be meeting. The other important genre to the guitar jam group were the handouts with song chords and lyrics. I'm sharing an example of a song I brought to the group to show you what this genre looks like.

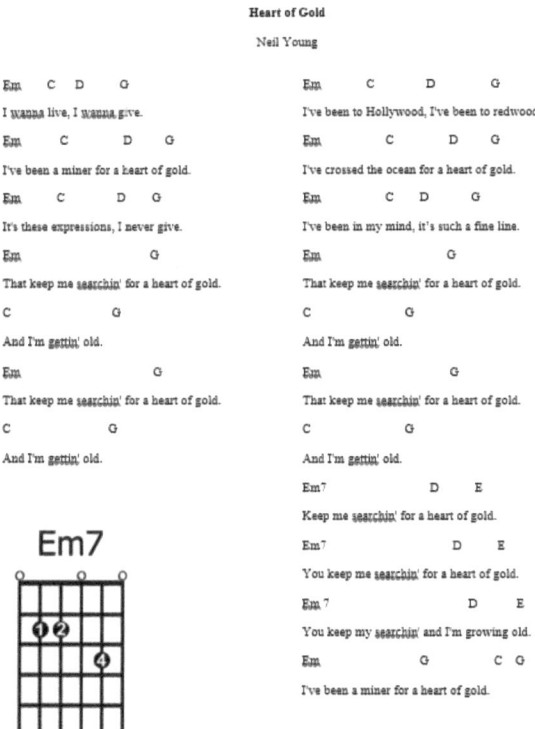

Figure 1: Lyrics and chord changes for "Heart of Gold" by Neil Young with a fingering chart for an E minor 7 chord

This genre of the chord and lyrics sheet was needed to make sure everyone could play along and follow the singer. The conventions of this genre—the "norms"—weren't just arbitrary rules or formulas. As with all genres, the conventions developed because of the social action of the genre. The sheets included lyrics so that we could all sing along and make sure we knew when to change chords. The sheets included visuals of unusual chords, like the Em7 chord (E minor seventh) in my example, because there were some beginner guitarists who were a part of the community. If the community members were all expert guitarists, then the inclusion of chord shapes would never have become a convention. A great resource to learn more about the concept of genre is the essay "Navigating Genres" by Kerry Dirk in volume 1 of *Writing Spaces*.

A Specific Lexis (Specialized Language)

To anyone who wasn't a musician, our guitar meet-ups might have sounded like we were communicating in a foreign language. We talked about the root note of scale, a 1/4/5 chord progression, putting a capo on different frets, whether to play solos in a major or minor scale, double drop D tuning, and so on. If someone couldn't quickly identify what key their song was in or how many beats per measure the strumming pattern required, they wouldn't be able to communicate effectively with the community members. We didn't use this language to show off or to try to discourage outsiders from joining our group. We needed these specialized terms—this musician's lexis—to make sure we were all playing together effectively.

A Threshold Level of Expert Members

If everyone in the guitar jam was at my beginner level when I first joined the group, we wouldn't have been very successful. I relied on more experienced players to figure out strumming patterns and chord changes, and I learned to improve my solos by watching other players use various techniques in their soloing. The most experienced players also helped educate everyone on the conventions of the group (the "norms" of how the group interacted). These conventions included everyone playing in the same key, everyone taking turns playing solo lead guitar, and everyone bringing songs to play. But discourse community conventions aren't always just about maintaining group harmony. In most discourse communities, new members can also expand the knowledge and genres of the community. For example, I shared songs that no one had brought before, and that expanded the community's base of knowledge.

Why the Concept of Discourse Communities Matters for College Writing

When I was an undergraduate at the University of Florida, I didn't understand that each academic discipline I took courses in to complete the requirements of my degree (history, philosophy, biology, math, political science, sociology, English) was a different discourse community. Each of these academic fields had their own goals, their own genres, their own writing conventions, their own formats for citing sources, and their own expectations for writing style. I thought each of the teachers I encountered in my undergraduate career just had their own personal preferences that all felt pretty random to me. I didn't understand that each teacher was trying to act as a representative of the discourse community of their field. I was a new member of their discourse communities, and they were introducing me to the genres and conventions of their disciplines. Unfortunately, teachers are so used to the conventions of their discourse communities that they sometimes don't explain to students the reasons behind the writing conventions of their discourse communities.

It wasn't until I studied research about college writing while I was in graduate school that I learned about genres and discourse communities, and by the time I was doing my dissertation for my PhD, I got so interested in studying college writing that I did a national study of college teachers' writing assignments and syllabi. Believe it or not, I analyzed the genres and discourse communities of over 2,000 college writing assignments in my book *Assignments Across the Curriculum*. To show you why the idea of discourse community is so important to college writing, I'm going to share with you some information from one of the academic disciplines I studied: history. First I want to share with you an excerpt from a history course writing assignment from my study. As you read it over, think about what it tells you about the conventions of the discourse community of history.

Documentary Analysis

This assignment requires you to play the detective, combing textual sources for clues and evidence to form a reconstruction of past events. If you took A.P. history courses in high school, you may recall doing similar document-based questions (DBQs).

In a tight, well-argued essay of two to four pages, identify and assess the historical significance of the documents in ONE of the four sets I have given you.

You bring to this assignment a limited body of outside knowledge gained from our readings, class discussions, and videos. Make the most of this contextual knowledge when interpreting your sources: you may, for example, refer to one of the document from another set if it sheds light on the items in your own.

Questions to Consider When Planning Your Essay

- What do the documents reveal about the author and his audience?
- Why were they written?
- What can you discern about the author's motivation and tone? Is the tone revealing?
- Does the genre make a difference in your interpretation?
- How do the documents fit into both their immediate and their greater historical contexts?
- Do your documents support or contradict what other sources (video, readings) have told you?
- Do the documents reveal a change that occurred over a period of time?
- Is there a contrast between documents within your set? If so, how do you account for it?
- Do they shed light on a historical event, problem, or period? How do they fit into the "big picture"?
- What incidental information can you glean from them by reading carefully? Such information is important for constructing a narrative of the past; our medieval authors almost always tell us more than they intended to.
- What is not said, but implied?
- What is left out? (As a historian, you should always look for what is *not* said, and ask yourself what the omission signifies.)
- Taken together, do the documents reveal anything significant about the period in question? (Melzer 3-4)

This assignment doesn't just represent the specific preferences of one random teacher. It's a common history genre (the documentary analysis) that helps introduce students to the ways of thinking and the communication conventions of the discourse community of historians. This genre reveals that historians look for textual clues to reconstruct past events and that historians bring their own knowledge to bear when they analyze texts and interpret history (historians are not entirely "objective" or "neutral").

In this documentary analysis genre, the instructor emphasizes that historians are always looking for what is not said but instead is implied. This instructor is using an important genre of history to introduce students to the ways of analyzing and thinking in the discourse community of historians.

Let's look at another history course in my research. I'm sharing with you an excerpt from the syllabus of a history of the American West course. This part of the syllabus gives students an overview of the purpose of the writing projects in the class. As you read this overview, think about the ways this instructor is portraying the discourse community of historians.

A300: History of the American West

A300 is designed to allow students to explore the history of the American West on a personal level with an eye toward expanding their knowledge of various western themes, from exploration to the Indian Wars, to the impact of global capitalism and the emergence of the environmental movement. But students will also learn about the craft of history, including the *tools used* by practitioners, how to weigh *competing evidence*, and how to build a convincing argument about the past.

At the end of this course students should understand that history is socially interpreted, and that the past has always been used as an important means for understanding the present. Old family photos, a grandparent's memories, even family reunions allow people to understand their lives through an appreciation of the past. These events and artifacts remind us that history is a dynamic and interpretive field of study that requires far more than rote memorization. Historians balance their knowledge of *primary sources* (diaries, letters, artifacts, and other documents from the period under study) with later interpretations of these people, places, and events (in the form of scholarly monographs and articles) known as *secondary sources*. Through the evaluation and discussion of these different interpretations historians come to a socially negotiated understanding of historical figures and events.

Individual Projects

More generally, your papers should:

1. Empathize with the person, place, or event you are writing about. The goal here is to use your understanding of the primary and secondary sources you have read to "become" that person–i.e. to appreciate their perspectives on the time or event under study. In

essence, students should demonstrate an appreciation of that time within its context.
2. Second, students should be able to present the past in terms of its relevance to contemporary issues. What do their individual projects tell us about the present? For example, what does the treatment of Native Americans, Mexican Americans, and Asian Americans in the West tell us about the problem of race in the United States today?
3. Third, in developing their individual and group projects, students should demonstrate that they have researched and located primary and secondary sources. Through this process they will develop the skills of a historian, and present an interpretation of the past that is credible to their peers and instructors.

Just like the history instructor who gave students the documentary analysis assignment, this history of the American West instructor emphasizes that the discourse community of historians doesn't focus on just memorizing facts, but on analyzing and interpreting competing evidence. Both the documentary analysis assignment and the information from the history of the American West syllabus show that an important shared goal of the discourse community of historians is socially constructing the past using evidence from different types of artifacts, from texts to photos to interviews with people who have lived through important historical events. The discourse community goals and conventions of the different academic disciplines you encounter as an undergraduate shape everything about writing: which genres are most important, what counts as evidence, how arguments are constructed, and what style is most appropriate and effective.

The history of the American West course is a good example of the ways that discourse community goals and values can change over time. It wasn't that long ago that American historians who wrote about the West operated on the philosophy of "manifest destiny." Most early historians of the American West assumed that the American colonizers had the right to take land from indigenous tribes—that it was the white European's "destiny" to colonize the American West. The evidence early historians used in their writing and the ways they interpreted that evidence relied on the perspectives of the "settlers," and the perspectives of the indigenous people were ignored by historians. The concept of manifest destiny has been strongly critiqued by modern historians, and one of the primary goals of most modern historians who write about the American West is to recover the perspectives and stories of the indigenous peoples as well as to continue to work for social justice for Native Americans by showing how historical injustices continue in different forms to the present day. Native American historians are now retelling history from the perspective of indigenous people, using indigenous research methods that are often much different than the traditional research methods of historians of the American West. Discourse community norms can silence and marginalize people, but discourse communities can also be transformed by new members who challenge the goals and assumptions and research methods and genre conventions of the community.

Discourse Communities from School to Work and Beyond

Understanding what a discourse community is and the ways that genres perform social actions in discourse communities can help you better understand where your college teachers are coming from in their writing assignments and also help you understand why there are different writing expectations and genres for different classes in different fields. Researchers who study college writing have discovered that most students struggle with writing when they first enter the discourse community of their chosen major, just like I struggled when I first joined the acoustic guitar jam group. When you graduate college and start your first job, you will probably also find yourself struggling a bit with trying to learn the writing conventions of the discourse community of your workplace. Knowing how discourse communities work will not only help you as you navigate the writing assigned in different general education courses and the specialized writing of your chosen major, but it will also help you in your life after college. Whether you work as a scientist in a lab or a lawyer for a firm or a nurse in a hospital, you will need to become a member of a discourse community. You'll need to learn to communicate effectively using the genres of the discourse community of your workplace, and this might mean asking questions of more experienced discourse community members, analyzing models of the types of genres you're expected to use to communicate, and thinking about the most effective style, tone, format, and structure for your audience and purpose. Some workplaces have guidelines for how to write in the genres of the discourse community, and some workplaces will initiate you to their genres by trial and error. But hopefully now that you've read this essay, you'll have a better idea of what kinds of questions to ask to help you become an effective communicator in a new discourse community. I'll end this essay with a list of questions you can ask yourself whenever you're entering a new discourse community and learning the genres of the community:

1. What are the goals of the discourse community?
2. What are the most important genres community members use to achieve these goals?
3. Who are the most experienced communicators in the discourse community?
4. Where can I find models of the kinds of genres used by the discourse community?
5. Who are the different audiences the discourse community communicates with, and how can I adjust my writing for these different audiences?
6. What conventions of format, organization, and style does the discourse community value?
7. What specialized vocabulary (lexis) do I need to know to communicate effectively with discourse community insiders?
8. How does the discourse community make arguments, and what types of evidence are valued?
9. Do the conventions of the discourse community silence any members or force any members to conform to the community in ways that make them uncomfortable?
10. What can I add to the discourse community?

Works Cited

Dirk, Kerry. "Navigating Genres." *Writing Spaces*, vol. 1, edited by Charles Lowe and Pavel Zemliansky, Parlor Press, 2010, pp. 249–262.
Guitar Hero. Harmonics, 2005.
Meetup.com. WeWork Companies Inc., 2019. www.meetup.com.
Melzer, Daniel. *Assignments Across the Curriculum: A National Study of College Writing*. Logan, UT: Utah State UP, 2014.
Swales, John. *Genre Analysis: English in Academic and Research Settings*. Boston: Cambridge UP, 1990.
Twenty One Pilots. "Heathens." *Suicide Squad: The Album*, Atlantic Records, 2016.
Young, Neil. "Heart of Gold." *Harvest*, Reprise Records, 1972.

Teacher Resources for Understanding Discourse Communities by Dan Melzer

Overview and Teaching Strategies

This essay can be taught in conjunction with teaching students about the concept of genre and could be paired with Kerry Dirk's essay "Navigating Genres" in *Writing Spaces,* volume 1. I find that it works best to scaffold the concept of discourse community by moving students from reflecting on the formulaic writing they have learned in the past, like the five-paragraph theme or the Shaffer method, to introducing them to the concept of genre and how genres are not formulas or formats but forms of social action, and then to helping students understand that genres usually operate within discourse communities. Most of my students are unfamiliar with the concept of discourse community, and I find that it is helpful to relate this concept to discourse communities students are already members of, like online gaming groups, college clubs, or jobs students are working or have worked. I sometimes teach the concept of discourse community as part of a research project where students investigate the genres and communication conventions of a discourse community they want to join or are already a member of. In this project students conduct primary and secondary research and rhetorically analyze examples of the primary genres of the discourse community. The primary research might involve doing an interview or interviews with discourse community members, conducting a survey of discourse community members, or reflecting on participant-observer research.

Inevitably, some students have trouble differentiating between a discourse community and a group of people who share similar characteristics. Students may assert that "college students" or "Facebook users" or "teenage women" are a discourse community. It is useful to apply Swales' criteria to broader groups that students imagine are discourse communities and then try to narrow down these groups until students have hit upon an actual discourse community (for example, narrowing from "Facebook users" to the Black Lives Matter Sacramento Facebook group). In the essay, I tried to address this issue with specific examples of groups that Swales would not classify as a discourse community.

Teaching students about academic discourse communities is a challenging task. Researchers have found that there are broad expectations for writing that seem to hold true across academic discourse communities, such as the ability to make logical arguments and support those arguments with credible evidence, the ability to use academic vocabulary and write in a formal style, and the ability to carefully edit for grammar, syntax, and citation format. But research has also shown that not only do different academic fields have vastly different definitions of how arguments are made, what counts as evidence, and what genres, styles, and formats are valued, but even similar types of courses within the same discipline may have very different discourse community expectations depending on the instructor, department, and institution. In teaching students about the concept of discourse community, I want students to leave my class understanding that: a) there is no such thing as a formula or set of rules for "academic discourse"; b) each course in each field of study they take in college will require them to write in the context of a different set of discourse community expectations; and c) discourse communities can both pass down community knowledge to new members and sometimes marginalize or silence members. What I hope students take away from reading this essay is a more rhetorically sophisticated and flexible sense of the community contexts of the writing they do both in and outside of school.

Questions

1. The author begins the essay discussing a discourse community he has recently become a member of. Think of a discourse community that you recently joined and describe how it meets Swales' criteria for a discourse community.
2. Choose a college class you've taken or are taking and describe the goals and expectations for writing of the discourse community the class represents. In small groups, compare the class discourse community you described with two of your peers' courses. What are some of the differences in the goals and expectations for writing?
3. Using Swales' criteria for a discourse community, consider whether the following are discourse communities and why or why not: a) students at your college; b) a fraternity or sorority; c) fans of soccer; d) a high school debate team.
4. The author of this essay argues that discourse communities use genres for social actions. Consider your major or a field you would like to work in after you graduate. What are some of the most important genres of that discourse community? In what ways do these genres perform social actions for members of the discourse community?

Activities

The following are activities that can provide scaffolding for a discourse community analysis project. To view example student discourse community analysis projects from the first-year composition program that I direct at the University of California, Davis, see our online student writing journal at fycjournal.ucdavis.edu.

Introducing the Concept of Discourse Community

To introduce students to the concept of discourse community, I like to start with discourse communities they can relate to or that they themselves are members of. A favorite example for my students is the *This American Life* podcast episode that explores the Instagram habits of teenage girls, which can be found at https://www.thisamericanlife.org/573/status-update. Other examples students can personally connect to include Facebook groups, groups on the popular social media site Reddit, fan clubs of musical artists or sports teams, and campus student special interest groups. Once we've discussed a few examples of discourse communities they can relate to on a personal level, I ask them to list some of the discourse communities they belong to and we apply Swales' criteria to a few of these examples as a class.

Genre Analysis

One goal of my discourse community analysis project is to help students see the relationships between genres and the broader community contexts that genres operate in. However, thinking of writing in terms of genre and discourse community is a new approach for most of my students, and I provide them with heuristic questions they can use to analyze the primary genres of the discourse community they are focusing on in their projects. These questions include:

1. Who is the audience(s) for the genre, and how does audience shape the genre?
2. What social actions does the genre achieve for the discourse community?
3. What are the conventions of the genre?
4. How much flexibility do authors have to vary the conventions of the genre?
5. Have the conventions of the genre changed over time? In what ways and why?

6. To what extent does the genre empower members of the discourse community to speak, and to what extent does the genre marginalize or silence members of the discourse community?
7. Where can a new discourse community member find models of the genre?

Research Questions about the Discourse Community

You could choose to have the focus of students' discourse community projects be as simple as arguing that the discourse community they chose meets Swales' criteria and explaining why. If you want students to dig a little deeper, you can ask them to come up with research questions about the discourse community they are analyzing. For example, students can ask questions about how the genres of the discourse community achieve the goals of the community, or how the writing conventions of the discourse community have changed over time and why they have changed, or how new members are initiated to the discourse community and the extent to which that initiation is effective. Some of my students are used to being assigned research papers in school that ask them to take a side on a pro/con issue and develop a simplistic thesis statement that argues for that position. In the discourse community analysis project, I push them to think of research as more sophisticated than just taking a position and forming a simplistic thesis statement. I want them to use primary and secondary research to explore complex research questions and decide which aspects of their data and their analysis are the most interesting and useful to report on in their projects.

8 The Evolution of Imitation: Building Your Style

Craig A. Meyer

Overview

This chapter focuses on incorporating imitation practices into a student's writing toolbox. By encouraging students to look more rhetorically at writing through imitation, they learn to recognize that language is more dynamic, and they can approach writing tasks with more contemplative thought instead of as a dreaded task. Through the use of structural and contextual imitation, students gain more insight into how sentences create meaning, how they can be changed, and how the decision-making processes relate to putting certain writing elements in certain locations for specific effects. While this article briefly touches on plagiarism as being distinct from imitation, students should recognize that imitation is not mindlessly copying, but mindfully understanding the rationale and effect of sentence structure, variety, and placement. They also learn how words form meaning within a sentence and, by extension, paragraphs and the overall paper. Imitation helps student writers realize that the more models, authors, and examples they can imitate, the more diverse and expressive their writing will become. Each time they understand how and why another author's sentence does what it does, they can use that insight in their own writing, which also increases their confidence.

Think for a moment on how you have learned most of the things you know.* Sometimes you learned by reading—perhaps from a textbook in history class. Sometimes you learned by doing something, like riding a bike. Sometimes you watched someone else and copied their

---

* This work is licensed under the Creative Commons Attribution-NonCommercial-NoDerivatives 4.0 International License (CC BY-NC-ND 4.0) and are subject to the Writing Spaces Terms of Use. To view a copy of this license, visit http://creativecommons.org/licenses/by-nc-nd/4.0/, email info@creativecommons.org, or send a letter to Creative Commons, PO Box 1866, Mountain View, CA 94042, USA. To view the Writing Spaces Terms of Use, visit http://writingspaces.org/terms-of-use.

movements, such as when you learned to write the alphabet. Oftentimes, we learn by mimicking or imitating others. Consider how you might catch yourself acting like a parent or close loved one—in essence, you are imitating that behavior. Your first reaction might be negative: "I don't want to imitate anybody!" And I think most people can understand that feeling. We want to be original. However, if we can acknowledge how much we can learn from other people's writing, then we can incorporate their experience and talent into our writing. In other words, we don't need to reinvent the wheel. Here, we will learn how to imitate another's writing and adapt it to our style, thus enhancing our own style to be more flexible and durable across writing tasks.

Learning by imitation gets a bad reputation even though we do it a lot in our lives. Imitation has mistakenly been linked to plagiarism. As you know, plagiarism is the copying of another person's work and not crediting them with it or taking credit for a piece of writing you did not write. For example, if you purchase a paper online and turn it in for a grade in a class—that's plagiarism. Likewise, if you copy a paragraph from a website and don't cite it, that, too, is plagiarism. Imitation is more complex than mindlessly copying down someone's words. Think of imitation as having a teacher that encourages you to figure out the hows and the whys something is the way it is—how to break it down, put it back together, and learn from that process to enhance your abilities.

To help illustrate, consider musicians. They listen to a lot of different types of music and each piece they listen to impacts their overall musical knowledge and experience. This influences how they create their own music. For example, I recall an episode of *Star Trek: The Next Generation* in which Data, the android (one who supposedly cannot create, just imitate; in fact, an imitation himself!), plays the violin. Captain Picard is called away and misses the concert but gets a recording of it. Later, this scene takes place between Picard and Data; they discuss Data's violin playing:

> *Picard*: The good doctor was kind enough to provide me with a recording of your concert. Your performance shows feeling.
>
> *Data*: As I have recently reminded others, sir, I have no feeling.
>
> Picard: It's hard to believe. Your playing is quite beautiful.
>
> *Data*: Strictly speaking, sir, it is not my playing. It is a precise imitation of the techniques of Jascha Heifetz and Trenka Bronken.

> *Picard*: Is there nothing of Data in what I'm hearing? You see, you chose the violinists. Heifetz and Bronken have radically different styles, different techniques, and, yet, you combined them successfully. ("Ensigns")

Data believes that the imitation and combination of two others is still an imitation in the strictest sense; however, as the scene makes clear, Data, by combining two "radically different styles," has created *his own style*. Without the imitation and interpretation of those two, he could not and would not have generated his own style; this is the power of imitation. That creation, then, becomes much more than mere imitation; it *evolves*. The evolution of prose is no longer an imitation of one, but of the combination of many to create your own. Although the scene depicted above refers to only two violinists, Data no doubt has heard dozens of violinists. Each one has left a mark on Data's performance and thus made *his* performance unique. Therefore, by understanding how others put words together and the style or voice of ourselves, we uncover a new set of procedures, styles, and possibilities, which then cease to be imitation but creation.

Our goal is not to *only* use imitation, but to consider it one of the tools of learning—a powerful tool, but *a* tool nonetheless. Yet imitation, as one of those tools, is different because it focuses on the improvement and empowerment of the writer through mimicry of another's style, voice, or pattern—not necessarily their actual words. Some time ago, I was reading *On Writing Well* by William Zinsser, and I hit a short section on imitation. Zinsser believes we must learn by imitation, and although Zinsser was a master writer, he continued to be influenced by other writers because all writers can continue to grow *as* writers. Each author a writer takes as an influence helps the writer grow and make stronger connections to words and phrases. Zinsser gives his take on imitation:

> Never hesitate to imitate another writer. Imitation is part of the creative process for anyone learning an art or a craft. Bach and Picasso didn't spring full-blown as Bach and Picasso; they needed models. This is especially true of writing. Find the best writers in the fields that interest you and read their work aloud. Get their voice and taste into your ear—their attitude toward language. Don't worry that by imitating them you'll lose your own voice and your own identity. Soon enough you will shed those skins and become who you are supposed to become. (235-36)

What he acknowledges is that as you gain more experience, you'll develop more of your own strategies to deal with the numerous problems you'll encounter when writing.

Here's our plan: we are going to look at a few pieces of writing and see what is happening so we might adapt it in our writing. We won't be copying or simply right-clicking to get a synonym, but learning from the style to improve our own. This doesn't mean we won't on occasion use some of the same phrases or words, because we will. But in doing so, we will be tacitly adjusting our understanding of how words make sentences, how sentences make paragraphs, and how paragraphs make papers. As our understanding of language interaction grows by looking at more examples, our style will become broader. Remember, writing is a continual process. We won't ever be perfect and we will need to continue working on our style by reading others and seeing how they make words work for them, then adapt that experience into our style.

We are going to consider two types of imitation: structural and contextual. First, structural imitation is mimicking the actual sentence structure of an author. We carefully look at how they put the words together to generate meaning and how sentences can be shaped to provide certain meanings. This form of imitation allows us to increase the variety of sentences we can utilize. Second, contextual imitation relates more to the style of a selected piece. By considering what, where, and why an author chooses to do something, we can understand the effect on the reader and why that choice was made. Here, we discuss both because both will add to our writing toolbox. Remember, our goal is to learn from other authors as we continue to improve our own writing and build confidence in our ability to handle writing tasks.

Structural Imitation

Let's take a look at structural imitation. A writer creates a sentence such as, *The windowpane protects me from the brutal world and its dangers*. Obviously, if you were not the writer, but copy that sentence exactly—it will never be *your* sentence. It will be the original author's sentence. Its generation or its reality was brought forth by that person. However, by imitating the structure, the impression of the sentence, we learn to imitate a slice of its original usefulness; it is this use that carries over into structural imitation, such as, *The explorer guided me away from the cliff's edge and certain death*. Even though I created both sentences, they are not identical. Yes, they have some of the same structures. Yet, the second sentence, even with my attempt to make them equal, is not the same. Imitation, then, in its purest form, is a new creation from an old model.

To help illustrate imitative sentence structure, let's look at some sentences below. You can also pick sentences from your favorite authors and imitate them for more practice.

- <Model> Writing with *real voice* has the power to make you pay attention and understand—the words go deep. (Elbow 299)
- <Imitation> Movies with great actors have the influence to make us believe and take part—the drama becomes real.
- <Model> I stared at the speaker in mute astonishment. (Poe 154)
- <Imitation> I smiled at my girlfriend in silent acceptance.
- <Model> In autumn, oak and maple and birch set up a blaze of color that flamed and flickered across a backdrop of pines. (Carson 1)
- <Imitation> On stage, strings and woodwinds and drums created a harmony of sound that filled and floated through the auditorium into the recesses of my ears.

In looking at these sentences, we probably notice patterns. Patterns are particularly useful and have been used to help many students. In their writing textbook, *They Say/I Say: The Moves that Matter in Academic Writing*, Gerald Graff and Cathy Birkenstein provide what they call "templates" that give us a number of these patterns. You can use these templates too, and, as you gain more experience, you can adjust them to fit your own style. Below are several examples from Graff and Birkenstein:

- While I understand the impulse to _____, my own view is _____. (309)
- Although X does not say so directly, she apparently assumes that _____. (311)
- X claims that _____. (312)
- The essence of X's argument is that _____. (314)
- By focusing on _____, X overlooks the deeper problem of _____. (314)
- X surely is right about _____ because, as she may not be aware, recent studies have shown that _____. (315)
- Although I agree with X up to a point, I cannot accept his overall conclusion that _____. (315)
- Yet some readers may challenge the view that _____. (317)
- My discussion of X is in fact addressing the larger matter of _____. (320)

These templates are more academic in nature than the earlier ones, and as you become more comfortable writing academic prose, you can adapt these to serve you better and more in *your* style and voice. For example, if I imitate the last template, but make it more in my voice, I might write, "This paper's discussion of X's argument focuses on the larger issue of _____." It's not a copy of the template, but you can see how it, more or less, leads us in the same direction. The point is other sentences give us a foundation on which to build.

These types of exercises drive us to explore how words work together and form a sentence and how that sentence works to create meaning. Sharon Crowley and Debra Hawhee, in *Ancient Rhetorics for Contemporary Students,* write that "imitation exercises ask you to try new approaches and to innovate within those approaches" (29). Indeed, imitation *becomes* innovation. One does not build star-shaped houses; they typically build square-shaped ones, partly because there is an abundance of models to mimic and they seem to be the most functional, but that doesn't mean they are all the same.

Contextual Imitation

Let's move to the other type of imitation. Contextual imitation focuses on the meaning and the many interpretations of that meaning. What a sentence's meaning is can be written several different ways. As we will see in the following example, every variation of a sentence can create new understandings and lead us into new directions. Take Desiderius Erasmus, who was a teacher in the 1500s. He provided his students with a simple sentence: *Your letter pleased me greatly.* Simple enough, right? How many different ways do you think you could rewrite that sentence?

Five? Ten? Thirty?

Erasmus generated 195! Some of his examples include:

- Your letter heaped joy upon me.
- After your note was handed to me, my spirit quite bubbled over with joy.
- I conceived a wonderful delight from your pages.
- All else is utterly repellent compared to your letter.
- At the sight of your letter the frown fled from my mind's brow.
- How delighted I was to read your letter!
- The happiness occasioned by your communication is greater than I can describe.

- I never set eyes on anything more gladly than your letter.
- Like clover to the bee, willow leaves to goats, honey to the bear, even so are your letter to me.
- Your epistle exudes nothing but joy. (*Collected Works* 349-353)

Each one of these examples is a variation of that original sentence; the context is what we are imitating. Certainly, we can assume that some of these might be unclear or even painful to read, but we can also assume that the context of how each one can be read is also slightly different. Erasmus is taking the original sentence and working through nearly two hundred variations, and in doing so, another sentence presents itself that can be used as a slight variation from the original. As we consider these samples, we see that the length is different, the verbs are different, even the term for *letter* varies. These variations provide more nuance and insight into the meaning of each one—even though, basically, they mean the same thing. By practicing this type of exercise, we flex our sentence-making muscles.

The other aspects of contextual imitation refer to the where and why authors make certain decisions in a piece of writing. To help explain some of this rationale, Donna Gorrell, who also champions the use of imitation, illustrates how those that use imitation are speeding up the process of learning. She explains that it demonstrates how other writers, when encountering a similar textual concern, find a way to solve the problem (Gorrell 55). In this way, instead of the tedious and time-consuming "[t]rial-and-error writing," we see how others handle a writing problem (Gorrell 55).

In what follows (see figure 1), we have an excerpt from a short creative nonfiction piece. As we look at the piece, focus on where the author is deciding to *do* certain things—the comments along the side offer some guidance to help us along. He is describing a baseball game during, what we learn is, a critical moment: the last inning, the author's team is up by one run, and he's the catcher. We pick up the action with an intimidating and athletic player on first base—called by the author "big boy"—and a batter having let pass two pitches:

The Evolution of Imitation   123

This newest batter was about my size and build with a Louisville Slugger in his hands. Every player knows that a Slugger is the bat of champions. He tapped his cleats with the mystical bat then readied his body to smack one beyond the fence. The first pitch he let go; it was a little outside and low. I could tell this was no ordinary moment, the crowd had hushed and I could feel tension in the air. I cautiously tossed it back to the pitcher. The second pitch was right on the money but he didn't bite on that one either. As I was kneeling back down after throwing the ball back, he deepened the trench beneath his right foot with his cleats, kicking dirt on my plate. GAME ON. Nobody but *nobody* kicks dirt on my plate; I shot back up ready to confront the transgressor. The umpire yelped, "Time!" and showed his backside to my teammates as he swept off the plate. Order was restored.

> **Commented [CAM1]:** This short end summarizes the entire paragraph; it shows that within the paragraph, there was disorder, but with the past tense, we see now it was restored.

I knelt back down and got ready to receive fastballs and curveballs. As the next pitch came, I saw the Louisville Slugger drawn back and begin to swing. The bat hit the ball with a crushing blow that sent it to my old homeland of left field. The runner on first took off like a rocket. The outfield was just getting a handhold on the ball as the runner whipped around second base. The third base coach was yelling, "GO, GO, GO!" to big boy as he neared third. The outfielder heaved the baseball toward me with I am sure everything he had. The ball bounced once and I caught it—solid. With the ball in mitt, I threw off my helmet and facemask. The runner had just rounded third and his coach in the dugout screamed "Bowl him over, bowl him over!" I clenched my teeth.

> **Commented [CAM2]:** Here the author ties his current position as catcher to his previous position in the outfield.
>
> **Commented [CAM3]:** This active use of the verb increases tension and heightens the action.
>
> **Commented [CAM4]:** The tension of the paragraph, as we see here, will carry over into the new paragraph with another short, powerful sentence.

I planted myself in front of my plate to defend it. As I tightened the grip of the ball, I could feel the stitches through the leather of my outfield glove. I looked into his eyes and he into mine, we both had an uncertainty, who was going to win? His mouth was open sucking in air, the crowd was still crying out, but I did not listen to them anymore. I widened my stance to cover more ground and lowered my left shoulder ready to receive whatever he had to offer. I took a deep breath and held it. As I waited, I could hear every crunch of his feet on the dirt mixed with the tightened pounding of my heart deep in my chest. Below my armpit, sweat ran down tempting me to laugh by its tickling gesture. I would have none of it. His arms rose as he began to dive headfirst into me like a linebacker in football. Big boy plowed into me like a tsunami hitting the beach. I could only hope that I held firm. His blow sent me off to the side onto my right elbow; we went down side by side, lying face to face on the fine gravel surface. Dust covered my tongue and clouded my vision. I felt dizzy.

> **Commented [CAM5]:** Here, as in the coming sentence, we see the pace dramatically slowed down to increase, once again, the tension set up by the end of the last paragraph. The author is slowing it down to increase our tension too.
>
> **Commented [CAM6]:** This reality of a distraction is quickly dismissed and heightens our focus on the incoming player, which enhances the readers need for *something* to happen.
>
> **Commented [CAM7]:** This violent image of a massive force hitting a stationary object helps balance out this paragraph from the earlier anticipation.
>
> **Commented [CAM8]:** After the collision, the pace returns to a slow, methodic one that is set up with details and the conclusion, again, summarizes the paragraph and sets up the next.

I did not know if I had stopped the run or not. My adversary jumped up and began to walk off to his dugout, as if nothing had happened. His face was expressionless, as if he got the run, but did not want to rub it in my face. A look of despair crossed my face as I realized I may not have stopped him. After several confused seconds, I rolled over to look at the umpire and he yelled with all he had, "OUT!" The crowd celebrated.

> **Commented [CAM9]:** With the dizziness of the collusion and now confusion of the score, our author is setting us up for a big win, or a big failure.
>
> **Commented [CAM10]:** Although not the end of the piece, this selection ends with a short sentence the gives a needed conclusion to the action of the preceding paragraphs. Short and powerful.

Fig. 1. Image of essay with marginal comments explaining some of the writer's rhetorical choices. Source: Craig A. Meyer, "Finding My Team."

This author, as we see by the comments on the right, decided to create almost a mini story at the end of each paragraph. This is a powerful technique (and one you can imitate). Think of it like this: imagine going to a movie that is two hours long. The first 110 minutes are horrible. You consider walking out but your friend insists that you stay, and she has the car keys. So you stay and suffer. But the last ten minutes feature the best piece of cinematography you've ever witnessed; it's exciting—these ten minutes of the movie bring everything together and ends with an unforeseen twist that you find brilliant and unforgettable.

As you're walking out to the car, someone asks, "So, what did you think of it?" What might you say? Still charged by the ending, maybe you explain how great it was, even though most of the movie was rubbish—the ending leaves the impression. In this baseball piece, the author wants to give us an impression at the end of each paragraph, and while you may not remember the details of the paragraph, you probably remember those short, powerful sentences at the end. That's the power of a strong ending. This technique of ending paragraphs with short, powerful sentences has just been added to your toolbox—you can imitate the technique to enhance your own writing.

In studying several authors or samples, we learn from each one's strengths and weaknesses. Imitation is more than just copying down a selection of writing—it's digging into the prose, pulling it apart, and understanding *why* it works the way that it does. More importantly, other scholars teach us *how they* write, *how they* combine words, phrases, paragraphs, and *how they* handle the writing problems they encounter. *Then*, we practice and transfer that understanding to our *own* prose. These exercises do not take over our writing; they become part of it and make it stronger. Just like Data, we can take radically different styles to develop our own style. The learning process derived from imitation takes time and dedication. Like many things, the process becomes easier with practice and persistence. Take the Erasmus example again; imagine writing a hundred different ways of telling someone you enjoyed their letter. Of course, that would take time and really focusing on the task at hand—it would not be easy. Yet, with each attempt to create a new version, something changes in us constructing it, and in that process, we stretch a little more outside the confines of the original sentence. It is this stretching where *imitative* learning takes place and it is how we grow as writers.

Works Cited

Carson, Rachel. *Silent Spring*. Houghton, 1962.
Crowley, Sharon, and Debra Hawhee. *Ancient Rhetorics for Contemporary Students*. 4th ed., Pearson, 2009.

Elbow, Peter. *Writing with Power: Techniques for Mastering the Writing Process.* Oxford UP, 1981.

"The Ensigns of Command." *Star Trek: The Next Generation*, written by Melinda Snodgrass, directed by Cliff Bole, season 3, episode 2, Paramount Television, 30 Sept. 1989.

Erasmus, Desiderius, and Craig R. Thompson. *Collected Works of Erasmus: Literary and Educational Writings 2.* University of Toronto Press, Scholarly Publishing Division, 1978. *EBSCOhost*, search.ebscohost.com/login.aspx?direct=true&db=e000xna&AN=468258&site=ehost-live.

Gorrell, Donna. "Freedom to Write—Through Imitation." *Journal of Basic Writing,* vol. 6, no. 2, Fall 1987, pp. 53-59.

Graff, Gerald, and Cathy Birkenstein. *They Say/I Say: The Moves that Matter in Academic Writing.* 4th ed., W.W. Norton, 2018.

Meyer, Craig A. "Finding My Team." *Composing Ourselves: Writing from the Composition Program at Missouri State University*, edited by Lanette Cadle and Lori Feyh, Moon City P, 2007, pp. 103-107.

Poe, Edgar Allan. "The Murders in the Rue Morgue." *Complete Tales & Poems of Edgar Allan Poe*. Vintage, 1975. pp. 141-168.

Zinsser, William. *On Writing Well: The Classic Guide to Writing Nonfiction.* 7th ed., HarperCollins, 2006.

Teacher Resources for The Evolution of Imitation: Building Your Style by Craig A. Meyer

Overview and Teaching Strategies

Authors have used imitation for centuries as a tool to improve their writing. This chapter focuses on using imitation to encourage students to look more closely at readings and learn to better explain how specific words, sentence structures, and sentence placement affects reading, which transfers over to how students write. As students practice imitation, they are gaining vital experience in flexing their sentence-making muscles and trying out various placements of prose that will improve their own writing. Through doing these, they come to realize that writing is more dynamic and allows for their own voice and style to come out.

While this chapter could be used at any time during a first-year composition (FYC) course, the earlier it is used, I think, the more practical use students will take away from it. To better engage students, ask them to bring in a favorite book or an academic article they thought was well written. These writings can easily be incorporated into the discussion of this chapter. Students can use them to practice imitation, which can then easily lead into a meaningful discussion about the differences between plagiarism and imitation. Near the end of the lesson, encourage students to discuss what they learned and how imitating an author's style will aid them in their own writing, while not sacrificing their own voice and style. The chapter also provides imitation exercises for students to do either as a class, in small groups, or on their own.

Discussion Questions

1. In what ways can imitation help improve your writing?
2. How is imitation different than plagiarism?
3. Name a few authors you've read. Describe their style as best you can. Then, go look and see how accurate you were. Then, look carefully at their style. Write down some examples of how you may be able to imitate the writing through structural and contextual ways of imitation.
4. Compare one assignment with other class members, pick out similar sentence structures or ways of explaining information. Discuss the patterns and why they are similar. What do you think led to

this similarity? How are the sentence patterns operating to drive the paragraph? The essay?
5. As a group, create a sentence (like Erasmus's) and generate as many possible variations. How are the variations similar? Different? What are the advantages in being able to present a sentence or group of sentences in many different ways?
6. As a group or a class, what other techniques could you learn from or imitate from the baseball selection?

9 Constructing Scholarly Ethos in the Writing Classroom

Kathleen J. Ryan

Overview

This essay offers a more robust definition of ethos than the typical definition of credibility to teach students more about ethos. I define ethos as the strategic positioning of the rhetor in relationship to the audience and/or community and then discuss four interrelated parts of ethos that can help students construct their scholarly ethos more effectively. The four parts—name your identity, commit to being a responsible writer, bridge gaps between the writer and readers, and locate your perspective—all emphasize ethos as social, relational, and dynamic. The chapter focuses on using these parts of ethos as interrelated heuristics to help students understand and develop their ethos across a range of writing situations.

Take a minute and imagine yourself doing each of the following:*

- Meeting your significant other's parents for the first time and deciding what to wear and what to say to make a good first impression.
- Interviewing for a job and trying to frame your prior job experience and demonstrate your work ethic to persuade the interviewer to hire you for a job you either really *want* or really *need*.
- Applying for a university scholarship and trying to persuade the committee members in a letter that your academic record and future plans make you the most deserving scholarship applicant.

In each of these scenarios, you have to make decisions about how to present yourself well to others by choosing what aspects of your life, work, and academic experiences to share to make yourself appear likeable, hirable, or

---

* This work is licensed under the Creative Commons Attribution-NonCommercial-NoDerivatives 4.0 International License (CC BY-NC-ND 4.0) and are subject to the Writing Spaces Terms of Use. To view a copy of this license, visit http://creativecommons.org/licenses/by-nc-nd/4.0/, email info@creativecommons.org, or send a letter to Creative Commons, PO Box 1866, Mountain View, CA 94042, USA. To view the Writing Spaces Terms of Use, visit http://writingspaces.org/terms-of-use.

deserving of a scholarship. In a sense, you're changing the face you show the world—emphasizing different aspects of who you are, what you know, what you've experienced, and what you believe— to best meet these different challenges. You're selecting what to say and how to say it. In each of these scenarios, you might share what you're majoring in, but you'll talk about it differently. For instance, you probably won't tell your partner's parents what your GPA is, but you may have to include it in your scholarship application letter, or it may come up in your job interview, especially if the job pertains, even loosely, to your major. You're likely to dress formally for a job interview in an office setting, but less so for one where you'll be doing landscaping or firefighting. When meeting your significant other's parents, you may want to look attractive, but probably not provocative. You're not lying about who you are and what you've done, but you are emphasizing different aspects of your character, abilities, and experiences to best suit the situation.

You may not realize it, but you're thinking about ethos when you're making these decisions. Ethos often gets defined as good character, credibility, and believability—concepts you may have encountered in a high school writing or literature class. And while these words and the scenarios above offer a pretty good start at defining ethos, figuring out *how* to achieve these qualities in a written text can be challenging, particularly when you're negotiating college writing expectations. This essay offers you a more robust definition of ethos, as well as specific strategies for constructing ethos as a part of your writing process. More specifically, I'll introduce you to a definition of ethos that focuses on how the relationships you make with readers in different writing circumstances matter. I define ethos as the *strategic positioning of the rhetor in relationship to the audience and/or community*. I use "strategic positioning" to indicate the way you're making deliberate decisions or taking specific stances in relation to others. I use the words "audience" and "community" to invite you to consider the different relationships you might cultivate with readers. You might imagine yourself writing *to* an audience when writing a research proposal you want approved or you might feel like you're writing *up* to readers who know more than you about your subject, but you're always writing *within* the context of a community, whether it's your actual classmates or an invoked community of writers or perhaps people with a shared interest in an issue or topic. I invite you to use this definition to help you make decisions to best help readers adopt or entertain your purpose more readily.

At the outset, I also want to make two additional points clear, and I turn to Jimmie Killingsworth's scholarship in rhetoric to help me. He writes, "The author's position is not simply a personal account of himself or herself. The author is a complex individual who selectively reveals (or creates—or conceals) aspects of character pertinent to the rhetorical work required at the moment" (27).

First, ethos is a construction; that is, ethos is not a representation of your whole self for readers, but a chosen or selected version of a self or persona fitting for that writing occasion. Second, a writer changes how they construct their ethos—what they "reveal," "create" or "conceal" to fit different writing situations. These two points imply you have the ability to learn to make decisions about how to present aspects of your writerly self to others, much as you might in the circumstances I asked you to think about in the opening of this essay. I want to help you understand and use that power better.

Below, I explain in greater detail what it means to define ethos as a positioning of the writer in relationship to audiences or within communities through your writing. You'll see this definition has four interrelated dimensions: the writer names their identity, commits to being a responsible writer, seeks to bridge gaps between the writer and readers' values or assert shared values, and locates their perspective in space and place. Becoming familiar with these four interrelated parts of ethos can help you better understand what it means to construct your ethos effectively. I've learned from working with my own students that if you have a more robust definition of ethos and more strategies for constructing your ethos in scholarly texts, you'll be able to understand and use this concept better, and even feel more connected to the writing you're doing and thus be more successful in your writing assignments.

Naming Your Identity

Naming your identity doesn't mean trying to account for your whole identity in any given writing assignment, since you're crafting what we might call a version of yourself on the page. It does mean offering details about *relevant* racial, ethnic, political, class, gender, and age (and so on) identifications and affiliations, like your membership in an organization, sport, religion or academic status (year, major, specific coursework) in your text. How do you know what is relevant? When one or more of the ways you identify yourself socially or you affiliate yourself with a group or principle pertaining to your topic, your purpose, or your relationship with your audience. Typically, it's most effective to highlight ways you identify with your readers and ways they can likewise identify with you, pointing out the ways you and your readers share similarities via what's called consubstantiality or identification. For example, one of my former students identified herself as a native of Libby, Montana, in the context of a research paper on the asbestos poisoning in her hometown; she used this aspect of her identity to give weight to her argument because she has firsthand familial anecdotes regarding asbestos-related cancers in addition to her researched evidence.

Here's an extended example to give you an idea of what naming your identity might look like in writing. One of my former students, Molly Williams, recently introduced me to an issue with wild horses in the western United States in her essay "America's Wild Horse Problem." As I learned from Molly, while the 1971 Wild Free Roaming Horses and Burros Act allows wild horses and burros to roam freely on public lands, the U.S. Bureau of Land Management rounds up wild horses by helicopter to control their population. They adopt them out, auction them off, or slaughter them largely because ranchers who want to graze their cattle on the same land view the wild horses as competition for food. The ranchers have a more powerful voice than those who might speak for the wild horses and burros. Molly wrote an analysis paper about this issue, focusing on an image that shows some of the violence and stress horses face in these round ups. In the paper, Molly didn't mention the particular commitment or identification she has with the issue, but she did write me this note at the end of her paper: "This is a topic of interest close to my heart because I am a lifelong equestrian and have been long immersed in the many facets of the horse world. I am also the proud adopter of two Little Owyhee mustangs." In these two sentences, Molly identifies herself as a "lifelong equestrian" and someone who has adopted two wild horses. That is, she names a particular identity and a personal commitment relevant to the public issue she wrote about. When you're encouraged to think about naming your identity in writing, you no longer need to present yourself as if you're unbiased or uninterested in your scholarly writing; instead, you get to name your identity to help readers understand your perspective more, and you get to express your passion about a topic or issue.

If Molly wanted to keep working on the paper, I'd suggest she bring those sentences into it to appeal to readers who might also be part of the horse community and signal her knowledge and experience for those of us who aren't. For example, in her conclusion she writes, "This seemingly dramatic photo represents a reality in our nation today." This would be a good place for her name her identity in relationship to this "reality" by bringing in the two sentences above, or some version of them. She might write something like this: "This seemingly dramatic photo represents a reality in our nation today, and it is a reality I know well as a lifelong equestrian who has adopted two Little Owyhee mustangs." You don't have to put sentences like these only in your conclusion. In her second and third paragraphs Molly lays out the different groups—preservationists, animal rights activists, and ranchers—who have a particular stake in the issue of wild horses grazing on public lands. Naming her identity when she is identifying the stakeholders in this issue is a good idea; doing so allows her to show her relationship to them.

Sometimes students struggle to feel a sense of authority when writing for professors because the identity of student seems to hold less credibility than the identity of teacher. When I ask my students to write about their identities and the challenges they feel in regard to them, they often write about how being a student or being young deauthorizes them. As a result, they have a hard time confidently contributing to conversations on issues they care about since some people, including their teachers, friends, and family, sometimes assume they don't know enough about a given topic because they are young or still students. A slightly different way, then, to read Molly naming her identity as a "lifelong equestrian" is that she is asserting a particular expertise in relationship to her topic. Here is an opportunity for Molly to present herself as an experienced equestrian and adopter of wild horses in a situation where she's not an expert writer. That way readers are aware of her special knowledge and identification and read with increased respect for both her passion and knowledge. Likewise, if you're majoring in environmental studies and writing an essay about the status of wolves as an endangered species in Idaho or Montana in your writing class, then specifically naming your identity as an environmental studies student can help you build your ethos when your readers lack this specialized background. I often tell students that including a phrase like, "As a scholar in environmental studies, I argue..." is a simple way for them to indicate their special knowledge and commitment to a topic and increase their ethos as knowers.

It's important to note, however, that, as Nedra Reynolds writes, "Unchosen characteristics—such as skin color and social status—limit an audience's perception of a rhetor's *ethos*," so you do want to be careful about what you choose to reveal to readers (325). Once you tell readers you're an equestrian or an environmental studies student, they have expectations of you as a result. They may judge your claims and evidence in relationship to their own knowledge of the topic, especially if some of your readers turn out to have more expertise on the subject matter or identify as say, a cattle rancher and have a different perspective on grazing rights on public lands, or even the status of wolves. You raise the stakes when you claim your identity because you invite others to do the same. But that's okay, because we, your teachers, want you to care about what you write about and write with commitment. It's part of the power and responsibility of being a writer.

While these two examples are chosen characteristics, naming unchosen ones also shapes how others relate to you. You know this from living in the world in your visible, observable bodies—big or small, short or tall, black or brown or white. For example, writing explicitly as a member of a marginalized group, whether as a woman, a Native man, a sex worker, or a trans person, makes you potentially more vulnerable to attack by readers—not necessarily for the content of your writing or the validity of your arguments, but simply because of beliefs and assumptions some readers may project onto you. It's useful to consider how much you want to disclose about yourself in writing to encourage people to listen to you and to protect yourself. Of course, if you are writing to an audience who's very different from you in, for instance, religion or race, it's useful to recognize those differences if only to yourself because doing so will shape how you invent and develop your argument. In some contexts, audiences or communities might be more disposed to read a text where you share relevant aspects of your identity than others because they share or value those characteristics and perspectives, too. Likewise, naming your sexual orientation and/or race can also be an empowering way of naming your identity in order to claim the importance of your particular experiences. When sharing your writing with classmates, they can see some visible evidence of your identity through your body, or they might know about your interests as a peer, but as a writer whose readers are removed from your immediate context, you get to think carefully about the identities you name as a way to help you create relationships with readers, to create a scholarly ethos. Ultimately, naming some aspect of your identity can be a both a powerful and vulnerable move.

Being Responsible

Naming an aspect of your identity to readers may well, as I've suggested, encourage you to claim responsibility for that perspective. Ethos, Reynolds writes, is "a way of claiming and taking responsibility for our positions in the world, for the ways we see, for the places from which we speak" (336-7). I love this quotation because it teaches us that we are answerable for what we write, for the positions we take in arguments and for the stories and reflections we share in personal essays. You must strive to be a responsible knower, holding yourself accountable (as your readers will) for what you know, what you write, and how you write about it. Doing so will reinforce the power of offering your written perspective. A writer can persuade others to consider new perspectives or better understand where they're coming from, so you want to make sure you do this work thoughtfully. Did you notice, in the example above, that if Molly names her commitment to wild horses and her position in the paper, she assumes a responsibility for that position that goes beyond her paper? When I wrote that Molly raises the stakes in her relationship to readers if she brings those sentences about being an equestrian and owner of wild horses into the paper, I mean that she's accepting this responsibility in a writerly context. In naming her identity as an equestrian and owner of two wild horses, she is also claiming her responsibility as a wild horse advocate.

In addition to being responsible for what you argue, being responsible also means not being arrogant or oppositional in expressing your beliefs and composing arguments, but rather treating your readers with respect and compassion: "Aristotle defined ... good will as 'friendly feeling towards anyone as wishing for him what you believe to be good things, not for your own sake but for his'" (Pittman 44). Having good will doesn't mean agreeing with perspectives you disagree with. It means disagreeing respectfully and knowledgably, not, for example, using logical fallacies like *ad hominem* appeals that make personal attacks on others or simply attacking others' perspectives with the kind of derision we see so often on social media. Molly shows her respect towards ranchers in her paper by acknowledging their concerns: "Mustangs are costing ranchers money and hindering industry growth." Had Molly made a sweeping generalization about all ranchers deliberately harming wild horses and burros, or even ignored why ranchers see the wild mustangs as competition in her paper, she might have alienated this audience, including classmates who grew up on ranches with wild horse populations nearby, and would have shown readers a lack of awareness of the multiple perspectives on this issue. In other words, lots of strategies your teacher can share with you about making sound arguments help you be responsible towards potential readers and towards the issue at hand.

This past semester my students and I discussed a term that is relevant here: intellectual humility. Intellectual humility, according to science reporter Brian Resnick, invites us "to be thoughtful in choosing our convictions, be open to adjusting them, seek out their flaws, and never stop being curious about why we believe what we believe" (Resnick). Practicing intellectual humility describes a way to be ethically responsible as a writer and researcher. It invites you to interrogate your blind spots, do research to test your ideas and claims, but also think about how you write up that research. This kind of commitment extends to working honorably with sources, particularly being accurate with the evidence you use. Teachers dwell on the proper use of citations in texts and in works cited pages because citing, paraphrasing, and summarizing sources accurately are all ways of demonstrating you're a responsible writer when it comes to representing and talking about your source material. Developing a scholarly ethos entails recognizing the values of the academic community and engaging them as a writer. You're showing you take your responsibilities as a thinker and writer seriously. Being responsible means working to research and argue about issues you care about, like wild horses, with care and attention towards what you write and how you write it.

Bridging Gaps Between Writer and Readers

When you are deciding how to name your identity and commitments and demonstrating your responsibility in an essay, you are considering the relationship between yourself as a writer and your readers—the audiences you write to and the communities in which you engage as a writer. When you start to write a paper, there often seems to be quite a gap between your aims as a writer and the real or imagined readers of your paper, whether your audience is your classmates, teacher, other members of your campus community, or some other group of people. Thinking about your scholarly ethos is a way to help bridge the gaps in beliefs, values, and identities between yourself and your readers to help you be more persuasive. For example, if you're writing an op-ed to propose your campus community support a proposed smoking ban on campus grounds, you need to try to move readers' opinions and actions to be more in line with the position you advocate. And whether you claim the identity of former smoker, the grandchild of a tobacco farmer, or a nonsmoker who wants to avoid the dangers of secondhand smoke, you are claiming a relationship to your text and building a relationship with your readers.

Let's look more closely at how you might bridge this gap between writers and readers using the example of writing an op-ed to argue for a smoking ban on your campus. My campus instituted a smoking ban a few years ago, and it was a subject of classroom debate at the time. Once you have determined your position and purpose, you can think about the audience for your paper and your relationship to that audience. Who is your audience? What do they likely know and value about your issue? The audience may be your classmates or, if you want to publish your op-ed in your school paper, you might expand your audience to include students more generally, staff, faculty, and administrators in order to reflect the campus community more broadly. You might invoke a wider readership of students for your op-ed even if you do not publish your work in the school paper. Doing so invites you to think about the different identities of the student body and their diverse experiences, from residential to commuter status, or to their place of origin, which may include regions in the U.S. where tobacco is grown or other countries where smoking is more culturally acceptable. If you're thinking about the entire student body, chances are some of your classmates are smokers, and so you need to think about why, with all that we know about the health risks of smoking and secondhand smoke, people still smoke. What social issues or factors are in play for these smokers? What health risks might they be underestimating? Questions like these invite you to consider what roles your potential readers might play in how you select and shape the content of your op-ed as you think through their potential identities, values, and experiences.

In this analysis of potential audience members, Tita French Baumlin recommends you keep in mind that "ethos necessarily shapes itself in accordance with dominant ideologies" (231). In other words, commonly shared values in your campus community inform what values are at play for your potential audience members and whether the values you hold in writing in support of a ban will be easily accepted or significantly resisted by readers. Understanding the relationship between your values and your audiences' values gives you good information you can use to build connections between yourself and your readers in order to encourage them to listen carefully to your position. This kind of analytical work helps you determine possible relationships you might make with readers; for instance, if you're writing as a former smoker who understands the allure of smoking socially, what kind of rapport can you build with peers who smoke or vape and might be against such a ban based on values you once shared with them? Or, if you're a nonsmoker, how do you show your readers who are smokers that you're attentive to their perspectives, experiences, and values? On many campuses, international students tend to make up a significant percentage of smokers since their cultures may stigmatize smoking less; whether you're writing as a former smoker, smoker, or non-smoker, how you name your ethnic identity and your stance may then discourage or encourage some of your readers' willingness to be persuaded due to their cultural identifications. Additionally, many people say they smoke to reduce stress, so how might you talk about the value of reducing stress in relationship to not smoking on campus? As you can see, naming your identity and claiming your responsibility towards an issue requires you to think carefully about the metaphorical distances between you and your various readers, the values you may or may not share, and how you'll work to bridge those distances.

Locating Your Perspective

As the opening scenarios imply, you're always making decisions about how to construct your ethos in context, in spaces and places. Think also of Molly constructing her ethos as an equestrian in the context of the wild horse problem in the western United States, or how you might construct your ethos in taking a position on smoking bans, or even the feasibility of enforcing them, on your particular campus. Not only are the gaps in values, experiences, and knowledge between writers and readers metaphorical spaces, but identities and affiliations are also kinds of bodily spaces and locations you occupy. They are places you "stand" and positions you "hold." For example, as a white woman, my gender and whiteness are social positions I hold that inform my worldview, and the fact that I live in southwestern Montana also shapes my perspectives and interests. This may be evident to you in the examples I choose to share, which tend to focus on issues at stake in my southwestern Montana community. Rita Applegarth writes that in this way, "*place* itself offers a crucial resource that rhetors can use strategically to signal their participation in particular communities" (49). "Place" can refer to metaphorical relationships, individual positions, and geographical locations. When you construct your ethos, you locate yourself, your perspective, and your relationship to readers in the text; your text is a place where you and your audience or community come together. Michael Hyde describes the idea of a text as a meeting ground this way: you "invite others into a place where they can dwell and feel at home while thinking about and discussing the truth of some matter that the rhetor/architect has already attempted to disclose and show forth" (xxi). Texts—paper or electronic—are places where writers and readers meet, and, in the process of constructing your ethos, you're trying to help readers feel welcome in your text. In other words, you want them to feel willing to keep reading and learning from your writing. Naming your identity, claiming your responsibility, and trying to bridge gaps between you and your readers are all ways of trying to engage generously with your readers.

Genres can also be understood as places, and writing well in a particular genre also helps your readers feel comfortable in your text and with your ideas. Applegarth goes on to say that genres, quite simply "...[are] *places* where rhetors invent, communicate, and act" (44). Just as being in specific, physical places, like a studio or a writing classroom, help you know how to dress and behave, knowing what genre you're writing also cues you to ways to present yourself and craft your ethos and also teaches your audience about what they might expect about your text and gives them cues about how to engage your ideas. Knowing the form of a text helps us understand where we are and thus what some of the expectation for that form include. This is why we know that a line of sympathy cards that includes jokes about the deceased wouldn't be a very good marketing strategy. The jokes would disrupt the expectation of sympathy cards as a site for expressing condolences.

As a writer, you can learn about a particular genre by collecting examples and describing and analyzing the patterns you see. Doing this helps you understand what kinds of expectations the genre sets up between you and your readers. Let me give you an example based on a fairly common first year writing assignment: a review of a movie, an event, or a product. Last year one of my students, Jake Purlee, had an internship at Stone Glacier, a local backcountry hunting gear company, and he was thrilled to get this opportunity because he's an avid outdoorsman. As a writing major, he has written extensively about his experiences and ethics as a hunter, especially a bow hunter, regularly naming this identity and exploring and studying hunting ethics in a variety of projects. As Stone Glacier's public relations intern, Jake wrote press releases for new products, but let's flip that to think about how writing a product review can help you think more about genre as a location, or place, that helps you construct your ethos. As you may know from researching possible purchases or even writing your own, product reviews include criteria for judging the product as well as reasons to explain your evaluation of it. Personal experience and even comparison to similar products often form the content of the review. If you're writing a product review of a specific multi-day expedition pack intended for hunters who hunt on foot in the backcountry, then you need to consider what evaluative criteria matters, like comfort, design, and quality of materials. You need to be comfortable in and confident about your gear if you're ten miles in the backcountry scrambling up a scree field in the snow, hunting deer, elk, or sheep, and hoping to carry out some meat for your freezer. In this genre, mentioning your personal experience with the product signals your knowledge of and investment in the activity the product is used for. You might mention your own experiences wearing the particular pack for a multi-day expedition as a way to describe its excellent design that allows for quick access to your rifle, spotting scope, and tripod, or its comfort even when carrying heavy loads, like when you hiked out with a mule deer last fall.

A reader's expectation, then, of a product review is that you know that you need criteria and reasons for your evaluation of the product, but also that you can talk about the product with some authority as someone who has used it. As someone who isn't a hunter, I could probably write a passable review of this kind of pack because I know the genre well and because I can at least draw on my experiences with backcountry camping. However, Jake would do a better job, once he has successfully studied the genre in the ways I describe above, for a few reasons: he has a lifetime of experiences hunting in the backcountry, using different brands of packs, and making decisions about the best gear for his needs. He intimately knows the kind of weather, terrain, endurance, and skills needed to hunt with a rifle or bow in the backcountry, so he knows what he needs from his equipment. He personally knows the criteria hunters would use to judge a pack as well as the language they'd use to evaluate one, because he is one. That is, the genre teaches him what kind of content—criteria, reasons, evaluation—matters for a product review, while his own experiences help him determine what those specific criteria and reasons for liking or disliking a specific multi-day pack are. The genre therefore helps him locate and draw from his experiences in a particular way, quite different from what he might write in a press release or essay about a particular elk hunting experience. While the backpack might figure into a personal essay about a hunting experience as a detail, its quality takes center stage in the product review.

Taken together, these four interrelated aspects of ethos construction—where the writer names their identity, commits to being a responsible rhetor, seeks to bridge gaps between the writer and readers, and locates their perspective in space and place—constitute a robust definition of ethos. While this definition of ethos as a positioning of the writer includes the more familiar notions of good character, good will, and intelligence, these concepts are reframed to account for the fact that a writer constructs their ethos in relationship to their prospective or actual readers, and that no single rule for having good ethos works in all circumstances. For each writing assignment you do, you need to consider what kind of scholarly ethos is best suited for that particular assignment and your interpretation of its purpose, audience, and genre.

Now that you are equipped with an elaborated definition of ethos, I want to draw your attention to two key principles that undergird this definition and may help you better understand it:

1. *Ethos is social.* You always construct your ethos in relationship to others, namely your readers. When you're making decisions about how to establish your ethos, you must do so with an understanding of your audience, whether it's comprised of your classmates, a readership your teacher assigns, or a community an assignment or genre invites. Molly wrote to her classmates, assuming they were unfamiliar with the wild horse problem, and even though she was writing as a wild horse advocate, she paid attention to the fact some of her peers likely grew up on ranches and might have a different perspective. When my class talked through the smoking ban on our campus, we considered the different kinds of students in our community when thinking about our different relationships with the issue and our diverse hoped-for outcomes. And even when writing a product review of a backpack, you're thinking about what your reader cares about and needs to know about the backpack. In this case, you can assume that they care about comfort, quality, and durability, and that readers would welcome your experiences with the pack as a fellow hunter. What counts as "good" ethos depends in part on your audience or community. Anticipating or analyzing your readers' knowledge, experiences, and dominant values as they relate to the subject of your paper and the perspective you share can help you decide how to construct and forward your ethos.

2. *Ethos is dynamic.* You don't construct your ethos once for all time. It changes across time, space, and place; relationships with different audiences and communities; and different aspects of your identity and commitments that you highlight for different projects. While Molly's equestrian background figures in significantly in her argument about wild horses, it's not relevant to her other projects on the vaccination debate or on making sourdough bread. The day Jake told me he got his first elk while bow hunting, he emphasized how much he appreciated the credibility it gave his hunting-related writing. As his hunting experiences change and develop over time, the ways he names his identity and talks about his commitments and responsibilities will also evolve. How you express your ethos shifts as you move from one genre to another and as you move about the world gaining new experiences.

Consciously practicing strategies for constructing your ethos can, over time, become habits of mind—that is, ways of thinking that are so familiar that they have become integrated into your writing process. I encourage you to think about how you might name aspects of your identity, commit to being a responsible writer, bridge gaps with your readers, and locate your perspectives in genres as you work on your writing assignments. I hope you can see, too, how learning about how to craft your scholarly ethos for different writing assignments can also help you think about how to show your best self to your significant other's parents, how to present yourself and your experiences to have a successful job interview, or how to best share information about your past academic successes and your future goals to get that college scholarship.

Works Cited

Applegarth, Risa. "Genre, Location, and Mary Austin's *Ethos*." *RSQ*, vol. 41, issue1, Winter 2011, pp. 41-63.

Baumlin, Tita French. "'A good (wo)man skilled in speaking': Ethos, Self-Fashioning, and Gender in Renaissance England." *Ethos: New Essays in Rhetorical and Critical Theory*, edited by James S. Baumlin and Tita French Baumlin. Southern Methodist UP, 1994, 229-263.

Hyde, Michael J. "Rhetorically, We Dwell." *The Ethos of Rhetoric*, edited by Michael J. Hyde, U of South Carolina P, 2004, pp. xiii-xxviii.

Killingsworth, M. Jimmie. *Appeals in Modern Rhetoric: An Ordinary-Language Approach*. Southern Illinois UP, 2005.

Pittman, Coretta. "Black Women Writers and the Trouble with Ethos: Harriet Jacobs, Billie Holiday, and Sister Souljah." *RSQ*, vol. 37, issue 1, Winter 2007, pp. 43-70.

Resnick, Brian. "Intellectual Humility: The Importance of Knowing You Might Be Wrong." *Vox*. 4 January 2019. www.vox.com/science-and-health/2019/1/4/17989224/intellectual-humility-explained-psychology-replication.

Reynolds, Nedra. "Ethos as Location: New Sites for Understanding Discursive Authority." *Rhetoric Review*, vol. 11, issue 2, Spring 1993, pp. 325-338.

Williams, Molly. "America's Wild Horse Problem." 4 February 2019. Rhetoric and Civic Life, Montana State University, student paper.

Teacher Resources for Constructing Scholarly Ethos in the Writing Classroom by Kathleen J. Ryan

Overview and Teaching Strategies

This essay grew out of my experience working with new teachers who largely defined ethos as credibility and didn't have access to more interesting scholarship on ethos with students. I want to offer teachers an article they can read with students that draws on ethos scholarship from the 1970s and 1980s by scholars like Arthur Miller, Michael Halloran, and Nan Johnson and then from the 2000s by Michael Hyde, Nedra Reynolds, and Coretta Pittman. I've found scholarship on ethos as social, strategic and relational is so much more pedagogically compelling than the static ways ethos as credibility gets defined. My hope is to make ideas from ethos scholarship available to students in a usable way, so that they have a heuristic for constructing their ethos in a range of writing assignments or projects as they move through their composing processes in your classrooms.

Discussion Questions:

1. Write for 10 minutes about your personal connection to and/or personal interest in a current writing project. What difference does it make to think about your personal connection to writing that is more formal and academic?
2. Find an assignment you wrote for another class, past or present, and write about how you constructed your ethos in that assignment (consciously or not). What might you do differently now that you know more about ethos? What changes would you make if you were going to rewrite that assignment?
3. The author indicates that constructing your ethos is a powerful and strategic move in writing. How is constructing ethos empowering? What kinds of power issues are involved in crafting your ethos for a writing assignment?
4. How does the author of "Constructing Ethos in the Writing Classroom" construct her ethos? Discuss particular places in the text where she names her identity, demonstrates she's being a responsible scholar, and builds bridges with you as a reader. To what degree are these moves successful in engaging you as a reader? Explain your response.

5. Read an academic article in your major and write an analysis of how ethos functions in that article. What do you observe about the place of ethos in that field and genre? What kind of relationship is the author or authors creating with you as a reader?
6. Define scholarly ethos in your own words. How are you working to demonstrate your scholarly ethos in a current writing project?

Activities:

The following are invention and drafting activities students might do as homework or in class. The activities are drawn from different textbooks I've taught as well as scholarship I've encountered in my ethos research.

Invention Activity 1. Naming your identity and locating yourself in the world.

1. List your racial, gender, ethnic, political, class, age, religious, geographical, and historical identifications.
2. List your primary commitments, desires, and interests as a student and in your personal life (including work and leisure).
3. List organizations or communities you belong to.
4. List special knowledge or abilities you have.
5. Write a few sentences elaborating on your experiences with some of the items in your lists.

Once you've gotten started with a current writing assignment, return to this list and note which aspects of your identity most relate to your current project. Do a focused freewrite on those aspects of your identity that tie into the topic, question, or ideas you're exploring.

Invention Activity 2. Bridging gaps through audience analysis.

This activity is adapted from the audience guide in Janice Lauer, Gene Montague, Andrea Lunsford, and Janet Emig's *Four Worlds of Writing*, a textbook I used as a doctoral student. I like reframing this audience analysis as an exercise in thinking relationally about writers and their readers.

1. Who are your potential audiences? What do they know and value?
   - What kind of background and experience do members of my audience or community have? How does this relate to the issue I am exploring?

- What does my audience value most? How do these values relate to my issue? To the way I'm naming my identity in this assignment? How strongly does my audience hold them?

2. What reader role will I call forth, or invoke, for my audience?

    - What knowledge and experience characterize that role?
    - What are the values connected with that role?
    - What does my readers' role help me learn about my research question or the issue I'm studying? About what I need to discuss in my paper?

3. What does my role imply for my writing of the paper?

    - What is my relationship to the audience I will invoke? Am I a peer? An expert? A critic? A student? A concerned member of some shared community?
    - What gaps between my identity and location and my readers' will I need to bridge?

INVENTION ACTIVITY 3. GENRE ANALYSIS.

I love Anis Bawarshi's *Genre and the Invention of the Writer: Reconsidering the Place of Invention in Composition*, and this activity is drawn from an activity he modified from a collaborative book he was writing at the time. This adaptation brings in ethos as an aspect of genre study and invites students to consider what aspects of ethos some genres call upon.

1. Collect and study the situation of a particular genre.

    - Where does the genre appear? What contexts? What issues, ideas, or questions does this genre address? Who uses this genre? What identities or commitments matter to people using this genre? Why is the genre used? What purposes does the genre fulfill for them?

2. Identify and describe patterns in the genre's features.

    - What content is included or excluded? What counts as evidence? How are the texts in the genre organized? What are their parts? What layout or appearance is common? How/do writers name their identities? In what ways are writers demonstrating that they are being responsible? What kinds of things do writers

reveal about themselves and why? What do you observe about the language?
3. Analyze what these patterns reveal about the situation.

- What do the patterns show you? Why are the patterns significant? What do participants have to know, value, or believe to understand or appreciate the genre? Who is included/excluded? What values, beliefs, goals, and assumptions are revealed by the patterns? What content is considered most important? What actions do the genre help make possible? What attitude towards readers is implied in the genre? What attitude towards the world?

4. Explain how the genre patterns shape ethos.

- What expectations does the genre set up in regard to the relationship the writer has with readers? What kind and degree of content related to ethos is most/least appropriate to the genre?

Drafting Activity 1. Practice Naming Your Identity

1. Add one to three sentences to a draft of a persuasive paper to see how you can more strongly position yourself in your text. Share an aspect of yourself that is relevant to the topic at hand and reference a value you share with readers related to your topic as a way to both open your paper and set up your ethos.
2. Try to compose a parenthetical reference like "as a _____" and fill in the blank with a relevant phrase drawn from your listing invention activity (see above) to concisely share with readers some aspect of your experience or background that can help them identify you and consider how who you are helps them engage your text. You might also point to the role you see readers playing using a phrase that cue readers into the kind of role you are asking them to play: "Like readers who care about _____, I _____". These are two concise ways of placing yourself in text.

Drafting Activity 2: Getting Ethos Feedback from Readers

1. How do you describe the relationship I'm trying to create with readers? What in the text makes you think this?
2. Are there places in the text where you're confused or offended as a reader? Please explain.

3. How well do I use specific details to explain my perspective?
4. In trying to name my identity, have I shared information about myself that seems irrelevant? If so, where?
5. On a scale of 1 to 5 (one being the worst and five the best), how well have I done in constructing a good scholarly ethos for this assignment? Please explain.

10 Writing in Global Contexts: Composing Usable Texts for Audiences from Different Cultures

Kirk St.Amant

Overview

The international spread of online access means we live in an increasingly interconnected world. This situation means our students will likely write for audiences in different parts of the globe. Writing for such diverse audiences means addressing different contexts affecting how individuals perceive texts. Writing students can benefit from approaches that help them understand the reading expectations of other cultures. This chapter introduces the *globalized rhetoric* approach of identifying the reading expectations of other cultures and overviews how students can use this method to analyze audience expectations among different cultures when composing for them.

Introduction

The international spread of online access means we live in an increasingly interconnected global environment.* These connections encompass almost every aspect of life, from business and economic developments to social and political discussions to entertainment and leisure activities. This means you might one day find yourself writing for audiences located in different nations or from other parts of the globe. Your audience will comprise individuals who will likely come from different cultures or groups

---

* This work is licensed under the Creative Commons Attribution-NonCommercial-NoDerivatives 4.0 International License (CC BY-NC-ND 4.0) and are subject to the Writing Spaces Terms of Use. To view a copy of this license, visit http://creativecommons.org/licenses/by-nc-nd/4.0/, email info@creativecommons.org, or send a letter to Creative Commons, PO Box 1866, Mountain View, CA 94042, USA. To view the Writing Spaces Terms of Use, visit http://writingspaces.org/terms-of-use.

with different values, beliefs, and expectations from yours. These cultural factors can affect how these individuals perceive and respond to the ideas you share with them through writing. The better you understand these dynamics, the more effectively you can compose texts that convey information to individuals from other cultures.

Composing across Cultural Contexts

This international environment changes the composition context. While you might have written for different audiences before, chances are they came from the same culture as you. This means you could draw from a common set of cultural understandings—from historical examples to discussions of fundamental social concepts—to compose texts for these readers. Different cultures, however, can have different perspectives on everything from what constitutes a valid topic for a composition to how one should introduce and discuss certain subjects in a text. The better you understand such factors, the more effectively you can compose texts for audiences located in different parts of the globe.

Let's be honest: composing for audiences from other cultures can feel daunting. It's not an easy situation to address, and it takes time to develop the understanding needed to do it effectively. After all, cultures can have nuanced expectations of what constitutes an effective text. The *globalized rhetoric approach* can help you identify such factors and compose texts that better meet the expectations of audiences from other cultures.

Globalized rhetoric involves understanding:

- The culture of the audience for which you are writing
- The genre you are writing in when sharing information with that cultural audience

In this essay, you'll learn how to use globalized rhetoric to understand the ways cultural factors affect the expectations groups associate with an effective text. This approach focuses on *usability*. Specifically, it helps you create texts a cultural audience can use to achieve a particular objective—the reason for which they are reading that text.

Re-Thinking the Writing Process for Global Contexts

Globalized rhetoric focuses on three things:

- Rhetoric: How individuals organize information so an audience can use it
- Audience: The people who use/read texts in order to perform a task
- Genre: The formats into which documents are organized for effective use (St.Amant, "Globalizing" 50-51)

By addressing these factors, you can create texts a particular cultural audience can use in the context of their culture. The process involves asking certain questions in a particular order. The resulting answers can help you compose texts that meet the reading preferences and usability expectations of different cultural audiences.

Question 1: Who is your audience/for what culture are you writing?

All cultures have *rhetorical expectations*. The members of a culture generally expect messages to be structured in certain ways and contain particular information to be considered credible or worth using (Campbell 36-44; Driskill 26-33). These expectations are deep-seated and exist beyond the language a person speaks. Thus, they affect how members of a culture view a message (i.e. whether it is credible and usable), regardless of the language it is in (Ulijn 80-81). This is important, for you might be using a common language—your native tongue—to craft messages for other cultures. But, doing so can lead to the assumption that strategies you use to present information in your own culture can be used with other cultures. That would be incorrect.

Here's the issue: cultures can have different perceptions of what constitutes a credible presentation of information (St.Amant, "Globalizing" 51-52). Cultures often use different rhetorical approaches to craft and evaluate messages. If individuals know the culture for which they are writing, they can research the rhetorical expectations that culture associates with credible messages and usable texts. Writers can use this information to craft messages that meet the rhetorical expectations of the intended cultural audience (Woolever 48-49).

Answering this initial question is the first step in the globalized rhetoric process of writing another culture. Cultures can have different expectations of how to use texts—differences that can cause misuse and miscommunication if not addressed. Once you know the cultural audience, you can use the following questions to learn about its rhetorical/reading expectations.

Question 2: What genre will you use to share information with that cultural audience?

Audiences rarely read randomly. Rather, they often use certain kinds of texts to achieve a particular objective. When you write for an audience from another culture, you are trying to produce a particular kind of text for that audience to use to achieve an objective. This factor of usability—or how easily individuals can use an item to achieve an objective—is central to determining rhetorical expectations.

Genres are standard forms of writing or conveying information (Berkenkotter and Huckin 1-2). When you write in a particular format, you are likely trying to create a certain genre of text. Genres are not random. Rather, audiences usually associate a particular purpose with a given genre. They read—or use—that genre to access the information needed to achieve an objective (St.Amant, "Globalizing" 50-52). For example, individuals use the genre of an instruction manual to access information on how to perform a process, or they use the genre of a movie review to determine the strengths and weaknesses of a film.

This genre-purpose relationship is key to usability, since differing cultural expectations of genres and the uses associated with them tend to create challenges. That is because cultures can associate different purposes with a genre (Campbell 36-44). Some cultures, for example, might associate instructional manuals with a product's marketing materials and expect manuals to contain information about the product's technical specifications in addition to instructions on how to use the product. Other cultures, however, could consider the purpose of an instruction manual only to present information on how to use a product. For these individuals, the addition of non-instructional technical information might seem unnecessary or distracting. So, writing for the genre needs of another culture involves understanding what those needs are because they are connected to how individuals plan to use the related text. To understand those needs, you must answer a series of related questions.

Question 3: Does the genre actually exist (and is it used) in the culture of my audience?

It is tempting to think because your culture uses a particular genre for sharing information that it exists in other cultures. This is not always the case (St.Amant, "Globalizing" 55-56). In fact, other cultures might not have or use the same genres that your culture does. Some, for example, prefer verbal interactions over written documentation to share information on different business activities (Woolever 56-57). As a result, the assumption you might need to use this genre to share information could be inaccurate depending on the culture of your audience.

Additionally, just because a genre exists in a culture does not mean members of that culture use the genre often—if at all. The genre of a Twitter post (a tweet) exists in German culture. Relatively few Germans, however, actually use Twitter (St.Amant, "Reconsidering" 16). As a result, such posts are not an effective mechanism for sharing information with certain German audiences.

These factors are important. If not known or considered, you could spend a great deal of time and effort creating texts in a genre your intended audience does not use. For this reason, writing for other cultures involves determining if the culture for which you are writing uses a particular genre. If not, you need to consider what other genres that culture might use to share certain information (e.g., using face-to-face discussions vs. written contracts to establish business agreements). Then, you can do a deeper review of genres to determine if you are using them effectively to share ideas. This situation leads to another key question.

QUESTION 4: IF THE GENRE EXISTS, WHAT PURPOSE DOES THE RELATED CULTURE ASSOCIATE WITH IT?

The same genre might exist in another culture. That factor, however, does not mean the other culture associates a similar purpose with that genre, uses it the same way to achieve the same objective, or expects to encounter the same sort of information in it.

Scholars like Charles Campbell and Peter Grundy have noted cultures can associate different purposes with the same genre (Campbell 36-44; Grundy 170-180). Anglo-Americans, for example, often use the genre of the business letter to convey information related to business processes. Other cultures, however, associate different purposes and uses with that genre. Certain cultures, for example, view the business letter as a mechanism used to display a knowledge of the recipient in order to establish a relationship with that person (Campbell 39-40). The idea is individuals from these cultures are more likely to do business with individuals who wish to form long-term connections vs. those who focus on short-term relationships. For this reason, they might review (i.e., use) letters to find some indication the writer has taken the time to learn something about the recipient's background – a gesture indicating an interest in creating long-term relations (Campbell 39-40).

Writers who do not understand such differences in use might fail to address the rhetorical expectations of a given cultural audience. This can result in the author's work being dismissed as non-credible, for it cannot be used as expected by the related audience. Writers, therefore, need to make sure they know what purpose and use a cultural audience associates with a genre. They can then take steps to meet such expectations and have their work seen as credible and usable by that audience.

Should you discover a cultural audience associates a different purpose and use with a genre, you need to ask certain follow-up questions (see questions 5-7 here).

QUESTION 5: WHAT KINDS OF INFORMATION DOES A CULTURAL AUDIENCE EXPECT TO ENCOUNTER IN THAT GENRE?

The purpose for which individuals use a genre affects another factor: the kinds of information one needs to present to meet the audience's expectations for that genre. If, for example, I associate the purpose of an instruction manual with providing information on how to complete a process, that manual needs to present information on that topic for me to use that genre as expected. If, however, I associate that genre with determining the quality of the related product, the manual needs to contain information demonstrating the product's quality (e.g., specifications on the abilities of the properties of the product) so I can use it to achieve that objective.

Failure to address such expectations can affect perceived usability in two ways. First, readers might think a text is not credible or usable because it lacks information needed to achieve the process for which readers are using the text. Alternatively, a text could contain information the reader does not think is essential within the context of a genre, because it is not associated with the objective for which readers use that genre. This situation could undercut a writer's credibility, since the writer could be seen as wasting the reader's time by presenting unnecessary information that affects how individuals can use that text.

Determining what information to include or omit is not easy. Expectations can vary from culture to culture. Also, the topics your native culture associates with achieving a particular objective in a genre (e.g., forging long-term relationships via a business letter) are not necessarily the same topics other cultures associate with achieving that same purpose in that genre (Campbell 36-44). For this reason, you cannot assume you know what information to exclude or include in a genre when writing for another culture. (This essay's next major section—"Researching Culture and

Genre Expectations"—provides strategies for identifying these genre-related factors.)

QUESTION 6: IN WHAT ORDER DO YOU NEED TO PRESENT INFORMATION IN A GENRE?

Cultures can have different expectations of the order in which one needs to present information in a genre for the related text to be considered credible (Driskill 28-29). Such factors reflect how the audience plans to use that text to achieve an objective. This means knowing the topics a cultural audience expects to encounter in a genre is not enough. Writers also need to know the sequence in which to present that information to make it usable for that audience. Failure to do so can cause confusion as audiences might consider essential information missing, only to find it at a later point in a text. Alternately, audiences might find certain information appears earlier than expected in a text; as such, they might not know how to contextualize that information because it appears in a sequence they are unfamiliar with and don't know how to use. In either case, such aspects affect the ability of the audience to use the text quickly and easily to achieve an objective.

These factors can include everything from the overall organization of a document and encompass what information to include in introductions and conclusions (Driskill 28-29). They can also occur at a more micro level and involve the order in which certain information appears within a paragraph. Such factors could even affect if writers are expected to note the connections between different items presented in text (like transitional sentences), or if information should be presented in seemingly disconnected chunks that require readers to intuit the connection among ideas.

These organizational differences can affect other aspects associated with the usability of a text. For example, where in a text should a table of contents appear? Is it in the front of the text before the introduction/body text, or is it at the end of the text, after all of the body text in the entry? That factor can affect how individuals perceive a text (that is, something is missing or is out of order) or how they use it (they cannot find information because they cannot locate the table of contents). Outlining the organization of a text prior to writing it thus becomes a matter of organizing information in the format in which members of the intended cultural audience expect to encounter it. Doing so should include accounting for the specifics (how are transitions among topics done?) and the generalities (what should be included in the introduction section?) of overall documents and genres.

Question 7: What visual elements should be included and how?

Visual elements are often expected in certain texts so readers can use them as needed or expected. In some cases, they provide examples of what something should look like (for example, the tools used to assemble an item). In others, they illustrate how to perform a process (such as drawings showing how to perform the actions described in a text). As with other genre aspects, the use of visuals in a text and the connections of visuals to usability can vary from culture to culture (Kostelnick, "Cultural" 182-184; Kostelnick, "Seeing" 31-33). Creating credible and usable texts for a cultural audience thus involves understanding and addressing expectations associated with the use and organization of visuals as well as with those of words.

Cultures can vary in terms of how much visual information they expect to encounter in a text. Some cultures might prefer more images in a space/related to a block of text than others (Fukuoka et al. 175-176). As a result, what constitutes a usable number of images per page for one culture could be considered overwhelming for another. Cultures can also vary in terms of what constitutes a credible and acceptable visual to represent something. In this case, using an image the related culture considers unacceptable or offensive could cause that audience to reject a text. In all cases, the issue is the usability of the resulting text—whether an audience can or will use it to achieve a given objective easily and effectively.

The nuances in such situations can be complex. Failing to address them can undermine a text's credibility, limit its usability, and lead cultural audiences to perceive documents in unintended ways. The more writers understand cultural-rhetorical factors, the better they can craft materials that address the expectations cultures associate with the usability of a genre. Gaining such insights involves researching the cultural audience who will use a given text. The next section of this essay overviews methods you can use to research the usability expectations a cultural audience has for a text.

Researching Culture and Genre Expectations

Understanding the rhetorical and the usability expectations of other cultures is not easy. Like any writing project, it requires you to do initial research on your intended audience. When doing so, you need to remember:

- Collecting information directly from your audience is key; you need to interact with members of your intended cultural audience to get the answers to the questions noted here.

- Cultures are not uniform; every culture contains different groups that have their own reading and communication preferences. You should never think, "I need to write a letter for individuals from culture X." Rather, be as specific as possible when researching your audience—e.g., "I need to write for 18- to 21-year-old college students studying at public universities in culture X."

Once you've identified the specific audience, you'll need to interact with members of that group to identify their expectations of genres, usability, and writing. Sometimes, you can do this via face-to-face conversations with individuals from that cultural audience. In other cases, you might need to use online communication technologies like Skype or Google Hangouts to interact with these individuals.

WRITING RESEARCH QUESTIONS

Regardless of how you interact with individuals, the overall research process is the same. It involves asking the following questions to members of the intended cultural audience:

- Question 1: Do you use [kind of genre] in your culture? (Next, see table 1.)

Table 1. Questions to ask and answers to consider when writing research questions.

	If "yes"	If "no"
Question 2:	What is the purpose of [kind of genre]—what kinds of information do you use it to convey, and what do individuals expect to use it for?	How do you share information about [process you want individuals to perform]?
Question 3:	What specific kinds of information do you expect to encounter in [type of genre] to achieve this objective/use it effectively?	What specific kinds of information do you expect to encounter in [type of genre] to achieve this objective/use it effectively?

	If "yes"	If "no"
Question 4:	How is information organized in [type of genre]; what information comes first, second, third, . . . last? [Use responses to previous question to determine how many pieces of information to organize.]	How is information organized in [type of genre]—what information comes first, second, third, . . . last? [Use responses to previous question to determine how many pieces of information to organize.]
Question 5:	Do you expect visuals to appear in [kind of genre]? If so, can you describe the visuals used, how many are used, and where on a page they appear?	Do you expect visuals to appear in [kind of genre]? If so, can you describe the visuals used, how many are used, and where on a page they appear?
Question 6:	Have you ever read American [or author's native culture] versions of [genre]? If so, did you find anything odd or that you would suggest changing if Americans [author's native culture] write for individuals from [respondent's culture]?	Have you ever read American [or author's native culture] versions of [genre]? If so, did you find anything odd or that you would suggest changing if Americans [author's native culture] write for individuals from [respondent's culture]?
Question 7:	Do you have any suggestions about writing a [genre] for members of your culture?	Do you have any suggestions about writing a [genre] for members of your culture?

These questions allow you to collect information on cultural expectations of rhetoric, genre, and usability. You can then consult this information when composing texts for the related cultural audience.

Methods of Data Collection

Two relatively effective methods for collecting answers to these questions are interviews and focus groups, but you can also use a mixture of these two approaches.

INTERVIEWS

Interviews involve meeting one-on-one with members of a culture, asking individuals the questions noted in the previous table, and collecting and comparing responses to identify commonalities in the answers received. But it can be tricky to determine how many individuals to interview. While more is better, realities of time, availability, and access to people from other cultures can create limitations. As a general practice, consider the "rule of threes":

- Responses from 1 person = personal opinion
- Common responses from 2 people = could be a coincidence
- Common responses from 3 or more people = likely indicates a trend

Based on this approach, if you can interview three or more individuals from the intended audience, you can begin to collect the information needed to identify cultural rhetorical expectations for a genre.

FOCUS GROUPS

Focus groups involve getting 3-5 people from your intended audience in one place and asking them to respond, as a group, to these questions. The idea is, group interaction can prompt participants to talk through and better reflect on and remember expectations for credible and usable communication in a genre. Unlike individual interviews, focus groups allow you to collect information from multiple individuals relatively quickly. Conversely, group interactions can lead to "groupthink," where the members of the group shift toward a group norm vs. individual preferences when conveying information. Ideally, you would use two or more focus groups comprised of 3-5 different people each time and compare responses across groups to identify trends. Achieving this objective, however, is a matter of the access you have to members of the intended audience and the time individuals have to meet as a group.

MIXED METHODS

You might also consider using *both* interviews and focus groups to collect information from the members of an audience. In this case, you could compare:

- Interview responses from different people to look for trends
- Focus group responses for each group and across groups to look for trends

- Interview trends with focus group trends to see if there are commonalities across both

Drawing from both approaches allows you to compare responses collected in different contexts. Such comparisons can help determine if consistencies in rhetorical and usability expectations exist across individual responses and group replies.

Medium of Interactions

It's best if you can meet with individuals in person to conduct interviews and focus groups. Yet this might not be possible. In that case, consider how you might use online media to interact with people in other nations. You could, for example, use Skype to do one-on-one interviews or a group Skype chat to conduct focus groups. Alternately, you could try to collaborate with someone in another country to organize an on-site focus group there and ask questions of the group via a technology like Google Hangouts.

On occasion, you might have on-site access to a very small number of individuals from a particular culture. In such cases, you might need to mix on-site and online interactions to gather multiple perspectives on cultural expectations. In the end, it is direct interaction with members of the other culture that is essential to gathering information on rhetorical and usability expectations. For this reason, technological options that allow for such contact can be an effective solution.

Final Thoughts

Writing in greater global contexts can be complex. It involves understanding the rhetorical expectations of other cultures—and of groups within those cultures—to craft messages they can use to achieve an objective. The globalized rhetoric approach can help you do this. They key is using certain methods to collect information on rhetorical and usability expectations directly from the members of a cultural audience.

By gaining direct answers to key questions, you can learn what other cultural groups consider credible, usable presentations in a genre. You can then use this information to craft messages that address these expectations. The more you know about your cultural audience, the better positioned you are to craft messages that audience will view as usable. In the end, it is a case of knowledge is power.

Works Cited

Berkenkotter, Carol, and Thomas N. Huckin. *Genre Knowledge in Disciplinary Communication: Cognition/Culture/Power*. Routledge, 1995.

Campbell, Charles P. "Rhetorical Ethos: A Bridge Between High-Context and Low-Context Cultures?" Niemeier, et al., pp. 31-47.

Driskill, Linda. "Collaborating Across National and Cultural Borders." *International Dimensions of Technical Communication*, edited by Deborah C. Andrews, Society for Technical Communication, 1996, pp. 23-44.

Fukuoka, Waka, Yukiko Kojima, and Jan H. Spyridakis. "Illustrations in User Manuals: Preference and Effectiveness with Japanese and American Readers." *Technical Communication*, vol. 46, no. 2, May 1999, pp. 167-176.

Grundy, Peter. "Parallel Texts and Divergent Cultures in Hong Kong: Implications for Intercultural Communication." Niemeier, et al., pp.167-18.

Kostelnick, Charles. "Seeing Difference: Teaching Intercultural Communication Through Visual Rhetoric." *Teaching Intercultural Rhetoric and Technical Communication*, edited by Barry Thatcher and Kirk St.Amant, Routledge, 2011, pp. 31-48.

—. "Cultural Adaptation and Information Design: Two Contrasting Views." *IEEE Transactions on Professional Communication*, vol. 38, no. 4, Dec. 1995, pp. 182–196.

Niemeier, Susanne, et al., editors. *The Cultural Context in Business Communication,* John Benjamins Publishing Company, 1998.

St.Amant, Kirk. "Globalizing Rhetoric: Using Rhetorical Concepts to Identify and Analyze Cultural Expectations Related to Genres." *Hermes - Journal of Language and Communication Studies*, vol. 37, 2006, pp. 47-66.

—. "Reconsidering Social Media for Global Contexts." *Intercom*, April 2015, pp. 16-18.

Ulijn, Jan M. "Translating the Culture of Technical Documents: Some Experimental Evidence." *International Dimensions of Technical Communication*, edited by Deborah C. Andrews, Society for Technical Communication, 1996, pp. 69-86.

Woolever, Kristin R. "Doing Global Business in The Information Age: Rhetorical Contrasts in the Business and Technical Professions." *Contrastive Rhetoric Revisited and Redefined,* edited by Clayann Gilliam Panetta, Routledge, 2001, pp. 47-64.

Teacher Resources for Writing in Global Contexts: Composing Usable Texts for Audiences from Different Cultures by Kirk St.Amant

Overview and Teaching Strategies

Aspects of culture and composition are often addressed at one of three points in a writing course:

- When discussing global contexts of writing
- When discussing writing for specific cultural audiences within the student's own nation
- When discussing online composition practices and the international access they allow
- This essay can be taught when examining any or all of these areas. By focusing on rhetoric and its use in relation to culture, the article provides students with a mechanism for examining cultural reading and writing expectations in a variety of cross-cultural contexts. When teaching this overall area, instructors need to make students aware that:
    - genre expectations are connected to the cultures using them vs. inherent to genres; and
    - cultures are not monolithic entities, but are comprised of diverse groups.

To this end, students need to learn the core idea that one doesn't write for culture X, but one writes for audience Y in culture X.

The globalized rhetoric framework described here provides students with an initial understanding of and a mechanism for examining the dynamics of these factors. Ideally, students will use the research questions and approaches noted in the entry to gain a better, broader understanding of such factors. The key is interacting with and collecting cultural-rhetorical information directly from the members of a specific cultural audience when composing for them. Instructors can use this chapter both to convey these ideas and have students test and apply related concepts in ways that enhance their understanding of such factors.

Discussion Questions

To help students explore the ideas discussed in these entries, consider having them address—as individuals, in small groups, or as an overall class—the following questions:

1. What genres do you use on an everyday basis and for what reason do you use them? What purpose do you seek to achieve when writing in or reading one of these genres?
2. What venues—on-site or online—do you currently use to interact with (or have the potential to interact with) individuals from other cultures? How might these venues be places where you might need to compose texts for those individuals? What kinds of texts would you compose and why?
3. The chapter provides a discussion of writing in terms of usability and how writing is used by readers to achieve an objective. Do you agree with this usability-focused approach to writing? Why or why not?
4. This essay discusses a particular approach to researching audiences from other cultures in order to create more effective texts for them. Do you think you could use this research approach when composing texts for readers from other cultures? Why or why not?
5. Could the approach—both the overarching questions and related research process—be applied to understand audiences within your own culture? If yes, how? If not, why not?

Examining these items can help students better reflect upon and consider how to apply the ideas presented in the essay within the context of their own writing processes.

11 Weaving Personal Experience into Academic Writing

Marjorie Stewart

Overview

"Warp and Weft" uses the metaphor of weaving to demonstrate one way of using personal and narrative writing within academic essays. Rather than debate whether narrative is appropriate for academic writing, it addresses the question of when is it appropriate and how it can be done effectively, focusing on helping writers decide when the use of personal experience is appropriate for their purpose, how to make personal experience and narrative pull its weight in the essay, and how the ability to incorporate personal experience can translate into the ability to incorporate research.

The essay is structured as an example of the use of personal experience as well as a how-to guide. "Warp and Weft" contains a discussion of three students who incorporated narrative in their essays in three ways: as a structural frame, as an example when the research topic and personal experience overlap, and as a tool for discovery. Students will benefit from the peer-written examples as well as the use of the personal in the essay itself.

Like many students, I worked my way through college with a retail job.* I was luckier than many of my classmates: I found a job at a hip little boutique called Rebecca: A Gallery of Wearable Art in the trendy part of town. We carried many styles of hand-made clothing, jewelry, and accessories, but our most important merchandise was that made by Rebecca herself. Rebecca was a weaver who made hand-woven clothing and scarves. Her loom took up half of the back room and she wove while I waited on customers. When one fabric came off the loom, Anne, the

---

* This work is licensed under the Creative Commons Attribution-NonCommercial-NoDerivatives 4.0 International License (CC BY-NC-ND 4.0) and are subject to the Writing Spaces Terms of Use. To view a copy of this license, visit http://creativecommons.org/licenses/by-nc-nd/4.0/, email info@creativecommons.org, or send a letter to Creative Commons, PO Box 1866, Mountain View, CA 94042, USA. To view the Writing Spaces Terms of Use, visit http://writingspaces.org/terms-of-use.

seamstress, would begin to cut and sew while Rebecca set up the loom for the next design. She created her patterns then transferred them into a computer program that told her how to thread the yarn onto the loom to produce the pattern. She threaded the warp, the yarn that runs lengthwise, onto the loom. The weft (formerly known as woof) was placed on bobbins that fed the shuttle. The act of weaving was moving the shuttle with the weft through the warp to create the weave.

So what, you might well ask. So what does this have to do with writing?

Many of you have been taught not to use the word "I" in your academic writing; not to include anything that does not directly relate to that mysterious thing called a "thesis statement;" and not to include anything personal in your writing. The opening of this essay has broken all of those so-called rules – it contains a personal story, told in the first person, that at first glance seems unrelated to the topic of writing. However, in this essay, I – yes, "I" – am here to help you step away from those rules and to use personal stories effectively in your academic writing.

The first consideration is whether using personal narrative is appropriate for your project. My story of working in Rebecca's shop is useful here – it is intended to attract the attention of the readers and to establish and explain the extended metaphor of weaving. However, if I were writing an essay for my art history class about the evolution of weaving techniques and equipment, my story would seem out of place, as I only have experience with one step in that evolution, and that experience is of an observer rather than a participant.

Your composition professor will likely talk to you about the rhetorical situation of any piece of writing. Stated simply (perhaps too simply), the rhetorical situation – the writer, the audience, and the purpose of the writing – affects the way the message is presented. In my hypothetical art history essay, the narrative would confuse the reader as to the purpose of the project and distract from the actual message of the paper. Often in writing classes it seems that your audience is specifically your professor and secondarily, perhaps, your classmates. Given the essays you will read about in this chapter, imagine the larger audiences that the student writers might have been addressing. Consider carefully whether personal narrative belongs in papers you are writing for history, biology, or business classes.

In addition to your specific rhetorical situation, of course, you should always comply with your professors' guidelines for each assignment. "No first-person narratives" is a clear statement that personal stories are not appropriate in that classroom.

However, once you have established that your narrative is appropriate for your purpose and audience, what next? It is my purpose to help you incorporate narrative effectively, and to do that, I will use examples from three of my students in a first-year course, a course designed to help writers bridge the gap between high school and college writing. I am also using the example of this essay itself. Consider my story about Rebecca. I am using her weaving, her design of warp and weft, as a metaphor for the kind of writing this essay is going to talk about. I will also use the story as a frame – talking about weaving in the introduction, the conclusion, and perhaps in the transitions.

Personal Story As Frame

Using a personal story as a frame for your essay can be an effective way to draw your reader into your ideas and then to help them reinterpret those ideas in the end. Perhaps, like me, you're working in a retail job. Perhaps it's in a big box store instead of my artsy boutique, and you're wondering if you'd be happier somewhere else, or you're thinking, please, hand-woven clothing? You sell electronics, important, functional electronics.

Just as I began with the story of my time at Rebecca, Lynn Z. Bloom began a conference presentation with a story from her classroom, and then commented, "Such stories, even brief ones, make us want to hear more, and to tell our own right back. They get us where they live. All writing is personal, whether it sounds that way or not, if the writer has a stake in the work" (1). One of my goals in telling the story of Rebecca is to make you want to hear more, and to make you want to tell your own. The human mind is a giant filing cabinet of stories, and when you hear one, you go to the appropriate file drawer – in this case R for Retail Employment – and pull out your own.

There are many stories in that drawer, however, and it's important that you choose the right ones. Because my metaphor of writing as weaving is central to my topic, I haven't included lots of other great stories that came out of my time at Rebecca. I didn't talk about the great gyros we used to get from Mike and Tony's across the street, or about how the changing nature of the neighborhood made Rebecca worry whether she had chosen the right location for the store, or about the great artists who came in for trunk shows of their work. I focused on the loom, the weaving. And as the framework for this essay, I consider the story of the loom to be the warp, the yarn threaded on the loom in advance. I will thread my shuttle with the examples of my students' writing and weave them through.

The first example, Callie Harding's "The Life of a Choir Director's Child," does the opposite. Her topic – the need for better education about religion in America – is the warp, and her childhood stories are woven though to show the reader how this topic became so important to her. Her stories give the readers context and help them connect with her.

Personal Story as Context

Telling a personal story can help your reader understand why you are writing about the topic you have chosen, and why you have come to care so deeply about it. Callie's childhood experience of travelling from church to church where her parents worked as choir directors gave her an understanding of many religions, and she uses those stories to show how that has helped her be a more compassionate, thoughtful, and sensitive person.

Her paper starts this way:

> When I was a child, I didn't spend much time on playgrounds or with the backyard swing set. I didn't look forward to dance class or soccer practice every week. Instead, most of my time was spent in the pews of a church with a My Little Pony figure that was weaving its way through a jungle of hymnals and pew Bibles. My playground was a cathedral with the somewhat harmonious voices from the volunteer choir echoing off the stone floor over the magnificent pipe organ. At the front of the choir was either my mother or father . . . Yes, I was the child of choir directors. (Harding 1)

Callie goes on to explain that her family moved from a non-denominational Christian church to a Jewish synagogue; the First Church of Christ, Scientist; a Catholic Church, and finally, a small Lutheran church. "What religion are we?" she asks. This is how she tries to answer her question:

> My mother spent a while with the Hindu faith before marrying my father and converting to Mormonism. We are also deeply into our Native American background and practice their cultural and religious ceremonies. Add the fact that we had many friends from many religions and cultures and you can tell that I had one of the most openly religious households on the block. (Harding 1-2)

Callie then moves very nicely into her research on how to encourage religious tolerance through education. She contrasts her experience in a fundamentalist Christian high school to a school district in Modesto, California where all ninth graders take a semester-long world religion course.

She writes about the importance of helping all children understand and celebrate diversity of religion and points to her own experiences as an example of the positive effect this has on them. As part of her research, Callie interviewed her mother about her diverse upbringing. While her mother called it a "happy accident," she also explained to Callie how she stood up to her very Mormon father to make sure Callie and her sister were free to find their own beliefs.

As I was studying Callie's essay, I took three highlighters and circled each paragraph: pink for Callie's personal story; yellow for Callie's presentation and discussion of her research, and green for the information from her interview with her mother. This is the result:

- Paragraphs 1-3 – Callie's personal story
- Paragraphs 4-6 – discussion of research
- Paragraph 7 – Callie's story
- Paragraphs 8-9 – discussion of research
- Paragraph 10 – Callie's interview with her mother
- Paragraph 11 – Callie's story
- Paragraph 12 – Callie's interview with her mother
- Paragraphs 13-14 – Callie's personal story

It wasn't until I did that exercise with the markers that I realized how smoothly Callie had incorporated the three elements of her writing. As I've done in this essay, Callie framed her story with the personal. She also used it within the essay to focus and reflect on her research findings. Marking your essay the same way can help you see if you have the right balance between the personal and the more traditionally academic portions of your paper.

While Callie used her personal stories to provide context to the issue of religion in education, she also used her own background to show herself as an example of someone for whom a broad religious education proved beneficial. In "A Life Lost," student Melynda Goodfellow used her personal story as an example.

Personal Story as Example

Melynda chose to write about teen suicide, certainly an important topic, but one that far too often leads to a patchwork of statistics and distant narratives, more a report than an essay with heart. Sadly, Melynda had reason to care deeply about her topic: her cousin Jared killed himself with an overdose of prescription pain medication.

Melynda started her essay with a simple story of a typical Friday night, getting ready to go to the high school football game, where her brother would be playing in the band. This night, however, was special, because her cousin had just moved into town and her boyfriend would be meeting him for the first time. Choosing to open with a typical activity – going to the football game – but giving it special meaning was particularly effective for Melynda. I encourage writers to ask themselves the first Passover question: Why is this night different from all other nights? This is the question asked by the youngest child at the beginning of the Seder to start telling the story of the Passover. It also serves the beginning writer well: If this night, this football game, isn't special in any way, then it isn't the story to use in your essay. Melynda's football game is different from all others because her cousin will be there to meet her boyfriend.

Although the atmosphere is festive, Melynda shows us with foreshadowing that this is not a typical Friday night lights story. She writes that Jared moved because "he wanted to get away from the lifestyle that he was living back home. He wanted a kind of fresh start." She connects herself to the characters of her brother and her cousin through the band: she had been in band, her brother is performing with the band at the football game, and her cousin is excited about returning to school and joining the band himself. Throughout the narrative part of her essay, Melynda shows Jared as sad and desperate, yet looking forward to his fresh start.

Melynda tells the story in a straightforward, chronological way from the evening of the football game through her cousin's death and funeral. Her use of personal experience is different from mine and Callie's because the majority of her paper is that narrative. The structure of her paper is very different: where Callie went back and forth between the story and the research, Melynda began with the story and introduced the research at the end. The first three pages of Melynda's six-page essay are the story of her friendship with Jared that fall, and how she becomes his confidant. Pages four and five are the story of how she heard of his death. It is only at the end of her essay that she introduces the statistics that show that suicide is "the third leading cause of death in people ages 15 to 24" (Goodfellow 6). Her conclusion, shortly after that statistic, reads:

> I never in a million years would have thought something like this would happen in my family. I knew that mental health problems run in the family, but I believed everyone knew where to get help. We knew that suicide wasn't an option and that we had each other

if nothing else. As tragic as it may sound, this event brought our whole family back together. Any quarrels or grudges anyone had seemed to dissipate that day. Ironically, one of the things that Jared wanted the most was for the family to just forget their differences and get along. (Goodfellow 9)

This ending refocuses Melynda's readers on the personal meaning of the impersonal statistic.

In his book *Living the Narrative Life: Stories as a Tool for Meaning Making,* Gian Pagnucci writes, "I think, actually, that stories can help us get at the truth even if there isn't a firm truth to be had." (51) And in *Writing to Change the World,* Mary Phipher says:

> Research shows that storytelling not only engages all of the senses, it triggers activity on both the left and the right sides of the brain . . . . People attend, remember, and are transformed by stories which are meaning-filled units of ideas, the verbal equivalent of mother's milk. (11)

Melynda works at getting at the true story of her cousin's death, making meaning of it, even though there is no firm truth or solid meaning to be had there. The truth she arrives at, however, is more powerful than the "just the facts" approach because the story lingers with her readers in a way statistics can't.

Another thing Melynda does that makes her essay different from mine, and Callie's, is her inclusion of dialogue. I think she makes especially good use of it in her essay, something that is often difficult for writers at all levels. Here she shows us how she learned of Jared's death:

> "What is it?" I said when I picked the phone up.
> "It's about time you answered your phone! I've been calling you for over an hour," my mom said.
> "Well?"
> "It's Jared. He's in the hospital. He overdosed."
> "Oh, my God . . . Is he okay? I'll be right there. I'm leaving work now."
> "No. Don't come here. There's nothing you can do. He's dead."
> (Goodfellow 4)

Recreating dialogue can be challenging – a year after her cousin's death, can Melynda be certain that these were the exact words that she and her mother spoke? Probably not, but she can show her readers the tension in the moment – her mother's anger that she didn't pick up, her desire to be with Jared, and her mother's postponing of the awful news. Dialogue also can be used to pick up the pace of the story – the light look of it on the page helps readers' eyes move over it quickly, getting a lot of information from a few carefully-chosen words.

There are significant structural differences between Melynda's essay and Callie's. Callie's is split almost evenly between personal experience and research; Melynda's is about 85% personal story. The third student, Ethelin Ekwa, uses personal story in an even larger portion of her essay, which is entitled "Ethelin Ekwa: An Autobiography." Although the title might lead you to believe that the essay is only, or just, or simply, personal narrative, Ethelin uses the story of her life to explore her ethnic heritage, her life as a single mother, and her determination to make the most of her artistic and musical talents. She tells the story of her life as a way of understanding her place in the world at the time of the writing.

Personal Story as Discovery

Ethelin's essay can be seen as an example of Donald M. Murray' beliefs about writing: "We write to think – to be surprised by what appears on the page; to explore our world with language; to discover meaning that teaches us and may be worth sharing with others …… . . we write to know what we want to say." (3). Although my students always write multiple drafts of all of their essays, Ethelin wrote more than usual – at least four significant revisions before the final draft that she submitted in her portfolio. She was a frequent visitor at our writers' center as she worked through the paper. Somewhere in an intermediate draft, she found her frame: a quotation from Ani Difranco's song "Out of Habit:" "Art is why I get up in the morning." That idea led her Ethelin to her conclusion: "I cannot imagine a day without the ability to create in unconventional ways" (Ekwa 9). In the eight and a half pages in between, she tells the story of her life.

In Callie and Melynda's essays, there is a very clear separation between personal experience, research material, and the writers' commentary on those elements. The weaving, to continue the metaphor, is done in larger blocks of color. Ethelin's essay has a more subtle pattern. Every paragraph contains some detail of her life – where she was born, who her parents were, where she lived – but also has a reference to her life-long desire to be an artist. She talks about her work as a writer and poet; as a singer and musician; and as a photographer and visual artist.

Ethelin's background is intriguing – her parents moved from Cameroon, West Africa to France and then to Texas, where she was born, the youngest of five children. She has lived in Europe and Africa, and she went to school in France and Cameroon. Here is how she introduces herself in the second paragraph:

> My birth name is Ethelin Ekwa. I am also known as Obsolete by my artist friends and as Krysty by my close personal friends. I am an artist, a mother, a photographer and a lover of all things. I am an American-born citizen with Cameroonian and French origins. I am 30 years old and I currently reside in North Braddock. (Ekwa 1)

Ethelin's identity is tied to her arts from the very beginning, and every story from her life is wrapped around those arts. When, at 22, she becomes a single mother, her priorities change, but she never gives up: "When I got pregnant, I put singing, painting, and drawing on hold . . . I had more pressing matters to take care of and there just was not time for art" (Ekwa 3). Soon, though, she tells us that she made a new friend who introduced her to digital photography, and by the time her daughter was two years old, she had her own photography business up and running.

While Melynda chose one special night to tell about at the start of her essay, Ethelin chose many events from her life, all of them important, life-changing events. Reading Ethelin's essay, I can almost see Rebecca's shuttle flying back and forth across the loom, the turn at each side another event that pulls Ethelin back into the world of art. When the weaver turns the shuttle at the edge of the warp, the weft creates a finished edge that prevents the fabric from fraying or unraveling called a selvage. The turns in Ethelin's story create a sense that her life, which is sometimes unplanned and chaotic, still has something that keeps it from unraveling, and that something is her artistic nature.

Tying Up Loose Ends

The examples from my students' essays can help you understand how to use personal experience in your academic writing. But how do you know when to use it? When is it acceptable and appropriate? Gian Pagnucci asserts, "Narrative ideology is built on a trust in confusion, a letting go of certainty and clarity that can ultimately lead to understanding" (53); that stories have a "piercing clarity" (17), and that "the drive to narrate experience is, if not instinctive, then at the very least quintessentially human"

(41). He also warns that the academic world is not always welcoming of personal experience. I know many of my colleagues are not willing to trust in confusion – their entire careers, and even their lives, have been built on the quest for knowledge and certainty.

If your composition professor has asked you to read this chapter, it's a pretty safe bet that you may use personal experiences in your writing for that class. Even in that setting, however, there are times when it is more effective than others. Using the examples of the essays I've quoted from and the guidelines given in the beginning of this chapter, here are some tips on when to use your personal experience in your essays:

- When, like Callie and Melynda, your experiences have inspired a passionate opinion on your topic
- When, like Ethelin, your personal experiences constantly point back to your central idea
- When, like me, your personal experiences provide a strong and extended metaphor for your subject
- When, like all of the writers, your personal experience provides a structure or framework for your essay

The expression "tying up the loose ends" comes from weaving and other fabric arts. When the yarn in the shuttle is changed, the new yarn is tied to the old at the selvage. Those threads are later woven into the fabric so that they don't show, and so that the connection is tight. When your rough draft is done, it's time to take the fabric off the loom and make sure your weave is tight. At that point, ask yourself these questions to be sure you are using your experience appropriately and effectively in your essay:

- What percentage of your essay is personal experience, and how does that match up with the nature of the assignment? Callie's essay was written in response to an assignment that required more research than the one Ethelin was responding to, so it included less personal writing.
- Have you included only the personal stories that directly relate to your topic, your attitude towards your topic, or your controlling idea?
- Are your selvages tight? Do the moves you make between personal story and research and analysis make sense, or is the fabric of your essay likely to unravel?

- Is the resulting pattern appropriate to your project? Are you working in large blocks of color, like Callie and Melynda, or the subtler tweed of Ethelin's essay?

I started this essay in Rebecca's shop and tried to weave the metaphor inspired there through this essay. In the process, I realized another advantage to using personal stories in academic writing: I hadn't thought about Rebecca and Anne, about Mike and Tony's gyros, about the bright creative atmosphere in the gallery and in the neighborhood for a long time. Accessing those stories from the filing cabinet in my brain was inspirational. My stories from Rebecca are mostly fun or funny. Your stories, like mine and the writers quoted here, are a mix of light and dark, funny and serious. I encourage you to open the file cabinet and find the stories that will make your readers remember similar times.

WORKS CITED

Bloom, Lynn Z. "That Way Be Monsters: Myths and Bugaboos about Teaching Personal Writing." CCCC 51st Annual Meeting, Minneapolis, MN, Apr. 2000.

DiFranco, Ani. "Out of Habit." *Ani DiFranco,* Righteous Babe Records, 1990.

Ekwa, Ethelin. "Ethelin Ekwa: An Autobiography." 3 Aug. 2009. Composition and Language I, Art Institute of Pittsburgh, student paper.

Goodfellow, Melynda. "A Life Lost." 3 Aug. 2009. Composition and Language I, Art Institute of Pittsburgh, student paper.

Harding, Callie. "The Life of a Choir Director's Child." 3 Aug. 2009. Composition and Language I, Art Institute of Pittsburgh, student paper.

Murray, Donald M. *A Writer Teaches Writing.* Rev. 2nd ed. Cengage, 2003.

Pagnucci, Gian. *Living the Narrative Life: Stories as a Tool for Meaning Making.* Heinemann, 2004.

Pipher, Mary. *Writing to Change the World.* Riverhead Books, 2006.

Teacher Resources for Weaving Personal Experience into Academic Writing by Marjorie Stewart

Overview and Teaching Strategies

This essay is useful for faculty teaching the research-based essays that are frequently the concentration in a second semester composition course in a two-term first year writing sequence. Instructors who encourage a personal connection to the research topic will find this essay helpful in guiding students as to when and how they might use their personal narratives in their academic research essays.

The questions below are designed to stimulate discussion and to move students from thinking academically about this genre to delving into their own lives for experiences they are inspired to research and learn more.

Often the attitude towards personal narrative, held by teachers and students alike, is that it is a beginning genre and an ice breaker that is designed as a stepping stone to real or more important ways of writing. This essay instead subscribes to the theory that personal narrative is, as Gian Pagnucci says, "if not instinctive, then at the very least quintessentially human" (41). My experience working with students on this kind of essay is that they are eager to both tell their own stories and to research the issues that inform those stories.

Questions

1. Marjorie Stewart claims that our minds are filing cabinets of stories. Do her stories, or the stories of her students, remind you of stories of your own? How does this chain of stories help us make sense of our experiences?
2. Has there ever been a time when you wanted to include personal experience in a writing project but were discouraged or forbidden to by an instructor? Why did you feel the story was important? What might have motivated the instructor?
3. Are their personal stories you are eager to include in an essay? What about stories that you would be uneasy revealing? How do you, and how do other writers, decide which stories they wish to share?
4. Work with an essay, either assigned in class or one you are familiar with in which the author uses personal experience. Compare it to an article on the same topic with no personal writing. Which do

your respond to more, and why? Does the personal writing help you understand the writer, or does it get in the way of your intellectual understanding of the topic?

Essay Resources

If you have a favorite example of a well-mixed narrative research essay, by all means, use it. If you are using a book with good examples, you might assign one as companion reading to "Warp and Weft." I also recommend many essays published as creative nonfiction, especially those from The Creative Nonfiction Foundation, at creativenonfiction.org. One of my favorites is "Rachel at Work: Enclosed, A Mother's Report" by Jane Bernstein, published in *Creative Nonfiction* and anthologized in their collection *True Stories, Well Told.*

12 Exigency: What Makes My Message Indispensable to My Reader

Quentin Vieregge

Overview

This essay defines the word exigency and explains its value as a way of gaining and holding a reader's interest. Exigency is defined as not simply explaining why a topic matters generally, but why it should matter specifically at this time and place and for one's intended readership. Four different strategies for invoking exigency are given with specific examples from student writing, journalistic writing, and trade books to clarify each strategy. Special attention is given to remind students of their rhetorical context, the interests of their readership, their readers' predispositions towards the subject matter and thesis (sympathetic, neutral, or antagonistic), and the possibility of connecting their thesis with larger issues, concerns, or values shared by the writer and his or her readers. The chapter closes with a discussion of how rhetorical uses of exigency differ depending on the genre.

Imagine someone browsing the aisles of a bookstore for something interesting to read.* This customer has an interest, let's say, for British rock, and, more broadly, popular music of the 1960s. After a few minutes, she finds a whole row of books, with titles about the Rolling Stones, the Beatles, and the British Invasion, but she only wants to buy one. She'll have to choose among them, deciding which book grabs her interest and which deserve to be tossed aside.

To make her decision, she'll ask a question that every reader ponders when opening a book, deciphering a poem, or reading a magazine article:

---

* This work is licensed under the Creative Commons Attribution-NonCommercial-NoDerivatives 4.0 International License (CC BY-NC-ND 4.0) and are subject to the Writing Spaces Terms of Use. To view a copy of this license, visit http://creativecommons.org/licenses/by-nc-nd/4.0/, email info@creativecommons.org, or send a letter to Creative Commons, PO Box 1866, Mountain View, CA 94042, USA. To view the Writing Spaces Terms of Use, visit http://writingspaces.org/terms-of-use.

"Is this text worth my time?" From an author's perspective, this question may sound sacrilegious: "Of course, it's worth your time, because I wrote it and poured over every word." But there's nothing more sacred to a reader than his or her own time (just recall the last time you had a paper with a fast approaching deadline and had to sort through a stack of library research). It's not enough to prove one's argument with irrefutable logic and overwhelming evidence; it's your responsibility to hold the reader's attention long enough for them to consider that evidence and logic. Inexperienced writers often assume that readers will have as much interest in a text's subject matter as they do, or they believe that the relevance of the text to the reader will be self-evident, but readers can be impatient, and must be convinced to read an argument before they can be persuaded to accept its thesis. It's the writer's job to clarify a text's relevance. Rhetoricians sometimes refer to this concept as a text's exigency, which may be defined as the circumstances and reasons why something matters—not only generally, but specifically at this moment, in this place, for this group of people (presumably one's readership). This essay will help you implement strategies to persuade your readers that your text is indispensable and that it cannot be put down, discarded, or be deferred until later.

Exigency in the Classroom

Now you might be thinking that the skill of evoking exigency might be essential for most writers, but not when composing school term papers. After all, you have a captive audience; the instructor must read your paper in order to grade it. She will have to read the entire text, and there's a good chance she's already interested in the subject matter. Furthermore, if your topic is chosen for you, then it's entirely possible you don't think that it's an absolutely essential or even pressing subject matter. Why bother, then, to make an argument sound enticing, especially if you may not really care about it anyway?

The answer to that question is two-fold. First, if there are twenty other students in your class writing papers over the exact same topic—or a closely related one—then you need every advantage you can get. Providing your paper with exigency will make the professor all the more eager to read it, which will improve her evaluation of it. Second, teachers will sometimes expect students to write to a more skeptical audience, someone who hypothetically could discard the paper or reject a weak argument, and they grade with this other audience in mind. The instructor will read your paper regardless of whether you provide exigent circumstances, but she will notice the difference between a paper that merely goes through the motions and one that proclaims, "read this because it will affect your understanding of an issue of essential importance." In a sense, your teacher is assuming a different persona—pretending to be someone else, in this case a skeptical reader—and expects you to do the same. However, the skill of invoking exigency isn't simply about earning a better grade; it's about captivating your audience and reinforcing the importance of your message, inside and outside of the classroom.

Strategies for Invoking Exigency in Writing

There are at least four strategies for invoking exigent circumstances in an argument. The first strategy functions as a type of umbrella for the other three. Let's call it "exigency through the audience's agenda or concerns," which involves igniting a spark of interest between your own thesis and your reader's interests. The other three strategies are variations of this approach, and the following examples will survey how some professional and student writers invoke exigency in different ways.

These four strategies illustrate that invoking exigency is more than just using an attention grabber or gimmick. An attention grabber is simply a way of turning heads; it's a visceral move that may work only temporarily, but exigency persuades the audience that they have a stake in your argument. The attention grabber focuses on flashy style, and no matter how effective it is, the best you can hope for is artificial engagement from your reader. Exigency concerns itself with subject matter, and its successful invocation makes readers care—or at least curious—about an issue.

Exigency through the Audience's Agenda or Concerns

To demonstrate that your paper has exigency, you first need to determine why you're writing. The immediate answer to this question might be, "because it's part of my grade," and though this response is technically correct, it will not inspire stellar writing. Instead, one of the best ways to answer this question is to assume a different persona. Think of a persona as a mask that you can put on or take off as a writer. It's a "think of yourself as" rhetorical move. You might think of yourself as a student in one paper, a scholar involved in an ongoing literary discussion in another, or an employee proposing a detailed solution to a corporate problem in another. Once you begin to consider your persona—and your reader's persona—you can start to form an opinion about why your paper would be important. Imagine that you were assigned to write a research proposal where you had to identify a problem on the campus that you attend and develop a solution to that problem. Your audience for this proposal would be whatever individual or group could effect the change you propose. So for example, if you were proposing different library hours, then your audience might be the dean of the library.

In the preceding assignment, you would need to begin thinking about how you, as a writer, could relate to your readers in order to take hold of their attention. That means asking some of the following questions:

- What type of persona do I have as a writer? What is it that I care about?
- What type of persona do my readers have? What do they value or find especially interesting? What common assumptions do they have, and do I share any of them? Do I believe any of their assumptions are false? What agenda do they have? What motivates them?
- What pressing, essential, or surprising issue may I, as a writer, share with my readers?

If we were to take the preceding prompt as an example, then you would be tasked with defining a campus dilemma and creating a workable solution that meets the needs of everyone involved—or at least as much as possible. You're writing to someone who could presumably solve the problem, if only she knew how. However, you still need to define a pressing issue and show how it demands your reader's attention. Let's say you decided to write instead about the lack of healthy food choices on campus (this student example is hypothetical; the other examples of student writing in this chapter are authentic). Your preliminary thesis sentence may look something like this: "The office of the dean of students should work with the Food Services Department to provide students with more healthy alternatives to the numerous fast food restaurants established on campus." That thesis sentence is clear enough, and a sympathetic reader might even already agree with you in principle: "Sure, I'm in favor of options; who isn't, especially if they're healthy." But simply because your readers agree with your thesis doesn't guarantee that they will be persuaded that something actually has to be done to effect change or even that they should read the rest of the argument. They might think, "But this is not a pressing issue, and furthermore, it's not my problem. It should be a long-term goal, so I'll wait to take a closer look at this proposal."

To capture your reader's attention, you should surround that thesis sentence with exigent circumstances that explain why this is an issue that matters here, now, and especially for your reader. This involves understanding and empathizing with them, so that you can connect their values with your agenda. Go through and methodically answer each of the questions above, perhaps building a table. Focus especially on finding out what matters to your reader on a daily basis, how they define their relationship to the topic you're writing about.

Table 1

Questions	Answers
What is my audience's persona?	The dean of students.
What is my persona?	A student (not simply a student-writer) who is concerned about an issue on campus.
What is my agenda?	In this case, I want to provide healthy food alternatives. I need to convince those with a position of power to assist me.
What values or concerns do my readers have?	After researching the job description for the dean, I found out the dean has a mission statement. The mission statement has yielded a connection, which will require explanation but will at least hold the readers' attention.

That way when you introduce your topic, you can meet them at their level, from their mindset. For instance, look at the chart above (see table 1).

Now that the persona of both the writers and readers has been thoroughly examined, the introduction can be written with an eye towards invoking exigency. The paragraph below represents how the thesis above may be merged with the additional contextual information in order to invoke exigency:

> The office of the dean of students at this university claims in its mission statement that it promotes a vibrant learning environment in part by "[collaborating] with institutional partners to address the needs of the student body" (*Dean of Students Office*). Furthermore, the dean wants to "support student learning" in part by "[reducing] barriers to student success" (*Dean of Students Office*). I applaud the dean's interest in how the entire campus experience can contribute to a student's ability to succeed and learn, but not enough has been done to provide students with nutritious options. Secondary schools across the country are beginning to provide ju-

nior high and high school kids with healthy meals, and researchers have well established a link between proper nutrition and learning potential. It's time for higher education to do the same. Therefore, I propose that the office of the dean of students work with the food services department to provide students with more healthy alternatives to the numerous fast food restaurants established on campus. I am convinced that the following proposal will live up to this university's excellent reputation of improving the daily lives of its students.

This passage demonstrates exigent circumstances by finding relevant research about a correlation between nutrition and learning. But, just as importantly, the student-writer researched the values and motivations of the intended audience, the dean of students. The student-writer matched language from the school's mission statement with the proposal that students should have more nutritious food options. Instead of the writer imposing an additional responsibility upon the dean's time and workload, the research proposal is framed as a way of helping the dean achieve his own goals. The tone is laudatory and encouraging: "I applaud the dean's interest" and "excellent reputation of improving the daily lives of its students." By answering the questions in table 1, the student has found a way to surprise the dean, showing him an added layer that complicates his mission of improving the learning environment.

Exigency Through a Gap in the Research

One of the most common methods for creating exigency in academic writing involves "creating a gap in the research," a well-worn phrase that most professors have heard and used numerous times. The strategy involves finding something new to say that contributes to an ongoing discussion. An academic discussion in this sense can occur over several years or even decades as each scholar conducts research and contributes knowledge to what has been previously written. After discovering a gap in knowledge, a writer must simultaneously show how his point is original but somehow still connected to what has been discussed or written by others. That might sound a bit contradictory, but it's precisely the same as walking in on an ongoing discussion. If you wanted to add to the conversation, you would first need to briefly listen to discover what the group is talking about, and then do your best to add seamlessly to the conversation, hopefully with your own fresh perspective. In everyday conversation, one might use transitional phrases like, "speaking of X" or "what you just said reminds me of Y." In academic literature, this strategy usually involves briefly reviewing what others have written and then pointing out what remaining question each of them has failed to answer. It might look something like this: "Though James Lewis has contributed X to the field and Adam Mitchell has contributed Y to our understanding of this issue, both have yet to ask how Z works."

Let's see how this approach might work in a student paper. The following paper is about the detrimental effects of media monopolies on the integrity of journalism:

> The dispute over media convergence and its effects on journalistic quality, motives, and localism has been the main focus of media professionals since the Federal Communications Commission (FCC) reformed its regulations on cross-media ownership in 2003. Since 1975, newspapers have been barred from purchasing television stations in the same market, in order to prevent news monopolies. Now, with the opportunity to deliver news across many platforms in a single market, management has shifted their focus from news content to audience reach, causing many to wonder if and when a compromise to the media's main objective as "public watchdog" will be shifted to meet the goals of improving their company's bottom line. "The questions that this transformation raises are simple enough….what should be done to shape this new landscape, to help assure that the essential elements of independent, original, and credible news reporting are preserved?" (Downie, Jr. & Schudson). Without the cooperation of the government, educational institutions, and media companies, it is almost certain that American journalism will continue to lose its focus, resulting in a three-ring media circus.

This passage does an excellent job of placing the paper's topic within a larger academic conversation. The introduction connects the writer's thesis to an ongoing debate about the "dispute over media convergence and its effects on journalistic quality, motives, and localism." Words like "dispute" emphasize the ongoing debate that scholars have about how Americans can reliably get their news. She does an excellent job of fitting herself within an existing debate with phrases like "has been the main focus of media professionals" and "causing many to wonder." These references to other writers clarify the relevance of the student-writer's argument by showing how her paper responds to problems or questions others have identified. It's like saying, "I've noticed you are very concerned about X; I have a thought about that subject too." If she only included those somewhat vague references to other writers, then the introduction would be weak, but the quotation from Downie, Jr. and Schudson introduces a specific pressing question that others feel must be answered. This specific question raises the urgency of her thesis. The thesis statement is no longer the student-writer's idle thoughts about a random topic; it's a specific response to an urgent question. In this way, using the "gap in the research strategy" provides writers with a purpose for writing and readers with an answer to, "So what?"

Exigency Through Reframing the Subject Matter

Exigency is not always invoked by explaining a gap in the current research; there are times when the best way to demonstrate a topic's importance is to redefine what the issue is about. You might think of this rhetorical strategy as "reframing" an issue. Writers reframe their subject matter by shifting our understanding of the surrounding context. In other words, it's a matter of what ideas, words, memories, or beliefs we associate an issue with.

Consider, for instance, an issue that arose in the summer of 2010 in New York City. A national controversy was spurred by plans to build an Islamic cultural center a few blocks away from where the World Trade Center Towers had been located before they were destroyed in the September 11, 2001 terrorist attacks (Fisher). These construction plans spurred debate about whether the cultural center was symbolically appropriate and whether it was an embodiment of American values or an insult to those values. Many people questioned whether it was appropriate for the Islamic center—sometimes referred to as the Cordoba house—to be placed near the location of a horrific terroristic attack (Fisher). Since millions of Americans who opposed the Islamic Center may have felt a sense of urgency about stopping its construction, a speech in favor of the center would face a particular challenge. The speech would need to address a skeptical audience, and it would need to convey a sense of exigency about why the completed construction of the Cordoba house was indispensable for America's future (the precise opposite of the audience's perspective). New York Mayor Michael Bloomberg made such an argument and crafted exigent circumstances by redefining the context (Bloomberg). Instead of people associating the Cordoba house with "ground zero," "September 11th," or religious effrontery, he needed them to associate it with America's long history of religious tolerance.

Bloomberg catches hold of his readers' attention by reframing the issue in at least two ways. First, he connects the topic of the Cordoba house to religious freedom from the founding of New York City in the 17th century. Early in his speech he states, "Of all our precious freedoms, the most important may be the freedom to worship as we wish. And it is a freedom that, even here in a city that is rooted in Dutch tolerance, was hard-won over many years" (Bloomberg). Bloomberg then reviews how Jewish immigrants, Quakers, and Catholics all faced resistance by others in New York. By connecting the recent Islamic controversy to similar past conflicts, he can argue that "[w]e would betray our values—and play into our enemies' hands—if we were to treat Muslims differently than anyone else" (Bloomberg). Only after reframing the debate from one about civic sensibility and 9/11 to one concerning religious freedom, can the mayor explain why his message is indispensable to his listener. He skillfully waits until the middle of his speech to confidently assert, "I believe that this is an important test of the separation of church and state as we may see in our lifetime—as important a test—and it is critically important that we get it right" (Bloomberg). His argument that the government should not prohibit people from worshiping as they wish could have been made without these exigent circumstances, but their inclusion changes the tone from one of a defensive posture to a more vigorous one. This example provides at least three lessons about exigency:

1. Sometimes it's best to invoke exigency in the middle of the text or even in the conclusion.
2. Consider delaying invoking exigency when a) your reader doesn't share your underlying assumptions, b) when your reader is unaware of the ongoing academic discussion c) when it's more important to leave your readers with a lasting impression than it is to grab their attention immediately d) when your thesis is placed in the middle or the end of your paper.
3. Whether reframing an issue or finding a gap in the research, exigency often involves connecting one's thesis with the audience's values. Reframing an issue involves the additional step of suggesting that readers focus on a different set of values than they otherwise would.

Exigency Through a Radical Reinterpretation of Knowledge or Experience

Sometimes writers try to surprise their readers with a bold claim, a counterintuitive idea, or a reconsidered foundational premise. Consider the following titles of bestselling books:

- *The World is Flat: A Brief History of The Twenty-First Century*, by Thomas L. Friedman
- *Everything Bad is Good for You: How Today's Popular Culture is Actually Making Us Smarter*, by Steven Johnson
- *The Wisdom of the Crowds: Why the Many are Smarter Than the Few and How Collective Wisdom Shapes Business, Economics, Societies and Nations*, by James Surowiecki

Each of these books tries to revolutionize the way that we think about their topics. The titles are crafted to provoke a confused but intrigued response: "What does the author mean by that?" "Is there something I don't know?" Bold claims can usually command attention, but only if the importance of the idea and its degree of innovation are properly established. Even if there is a radically new way of looking at something, it may appear quotidian. If you can appear to be turning the world on its head, unveiling an unseen world, or persuading people that up is in fact down, then you will have your readers' undivided attention.

Radical Reinterpretation in Student Writing

In the following exegesis of Wendy Cope's poem "Lonely Hearts," the student-writer proffers a counterintuitive analysis of the tone of the poem. On the surface, the villanelle appears to have a light mood that speaks of unfulfilled relationships, but a darker tone surprisingly lies underneath this initial interpretation:

> Solitude. It is a fear that has crossed many a mind for ages—the idea of being alone or, worst of all, dying alone. But is this loneliness individualistic in nature? Or does it serve to represent a tragic element of the human condition: to be in a constant search of companionship, an obsession so hard-wired that we often fail to see the bonds from person to person? These are questions explored by Wendy Cope in her poem "Lonely Hearts," a villanelle written in the form of pieced-together personal ads from a newspaper. On the basic level, "Lonely Hearts" amuses and entertains, seeming to

poke fun at those "lonely hearts" that place personal ads. But upon closer reading, the serious underpinnings of Cope's poem reveal themselves and a deeper theme emerges. Through the careful use of personal ad language, villanelle form, and ambiguity of point of view, Wendy Cope illustrates the shared loneliness of the poem's speakers that ultimately renders the poem ironic.

Can you spot how the student's introduction creates a surprise? There is a slow shift in her language from a theme of loneliness expressed with a jovial tone to one of "shared loneliness" (a term that is counterintuitive, itself) expressed with sobriety. The second half of the paragraph contains the thesis, but it's the first half that makes the thesis worth investigating. It invites readers to reconsider a poem that they have merely glossed over. It's like Alice going through the rabbit hole.

Genre and Exigency: Finding the Right Fit

Each genre has its own conventions and might easily fit with one of these strategies more than others. The word genre refers to a set of rhetorical expectations that accompany a recurring type of writing, whether it be practical or artistic. For instance, in business writing, there are rhetorical expectations that are associated with positive newsletters and a separate set of expectations for business letters that give people negative news. There are rhetorical expectations for emails, text-messages, news articles, poetry, drama, and even movie trailers, to name a few genres. Genre conventions are not hard and fast rules, but they do provide guidance. For instance, I would advise matching the genres below with the strategies to their right. Keep in mind these are merely suggestions. Any of the four strategies described above could work for any of the genres below, if creatively applied.

- Job Application Materials: Definitely "exigency through the audience's agenda or concerns" applies here. It's at the heart of any résumé or job letter. What you can do for the company is the only thing a potential employer cares about.
- Literary Analysis: "Finding a gap in the research" is the most common strategy, but reframing the issue or creating a counterintuitive idea are wonderful approaches as well.
- Business Proposal: "Exigency through the audience's agenda or concerns" is the most appropriate.
- Term Paper (where the topic has been discussed in class): With an ongoing discussion to references made in class, you could use any of the final three strategies.

- Term Paper (where the topic has been written about exhaustively or where the positions people take are predictable): This is the most difficult type of paper to write about (i.e. abortion, gun control, legalization of marijuana). Use the reframing technique or the counterintuitive technique to create a fresh perspective.

These strategies are oftentimes used simultaneously, and you may have noticed that there is some overlap between them. Though they may be nebulous categorizations, they provide a useful tool for providing a sense of urgency to your writing. I have personally found that when I think about exigency, it helps add passion to my writing, and it gives me a voice as a writer. Without exigency, I'm an aimless soul drifting in the dark night without a sail or a strong wind. But exigency brings with it a definition of who I am in the text (my persona), who my readers are (their personas), and the common bonds that connect use together. If you use these techniques it will help to animate your writing and motivate your readers to keep reading and carefully consider your argument.

WORKS CITED

Bloomberg, Michael. "Mayor Bloomberg Discusses the Landmarks Preservation Commission Vote on 45–47 Park Place." *NYC*, uploaded by The City of New York, 3 Aug. 2010, https://www1.nyc.gov/office-of-the-mayor/news/337-10/mayor-bloomberg-the-landmarks-preservation-commission-vote-45-47-park-place#/2

Cope, Wendy. "Lonely Hearts." *An Introduction to Poetry*, edited by X. J. Kennedy and Dana Gioia, 13th ed., Longman, 2010, pp. 61.

Downie Jr., Leonard and Michael Schudson. "The Reconstruction of American Journalism." *Columbia Journalism Review*, vol. 48, no. 4, Nov/Dec 2009, https://archives.cjr.org/reconstruction/the_reconstruction_of_american.php.

Dean of Students Office. University of South Florida, https://www.usf.edu/student-affairs/dean-of-students/. Accessed 3 June 2019.

Fisher, Max. "Is the Cordoba House Good for America?" *The Atlantic*, 3 Aug. 2010, https://www.theatlantic.com/national/archive/2010/08/is-the-cordoba-house-good-for-america/344631/. Accessed 8 September 2019.

Friedman, Thomas L. *The World is Flat: A Brief History of the Twenty-First Century*. Farrar, Straus and Giroux, 2005.

Johnson, Steven. *Everything Bad is Good For You: How Today's Popular Culture is Actually Making Us Smarter*. Riverhead Books, 2005.

Surowiecki, James. *The Wisdom of the Crowds: Why the Many are Smarter Than the Few and How Collective Wisdom Shapes Business, Economics, Societies and Nations*. Doubleday, 2004.

Teacher Resources for Exigency: What Makes My Message Indispensable to My Reader by Quentin Vieregge

Overview

Discussing exigency can help students to not simply think about the "so what" of their writing, but also to consider and analyze the prompt more carefully. I've found that students go through a layered understanding of a prompt, at first understanding the basic concept and then looking more carefully at the prompt's specific requirements. But what makes their papers far more effective is if they can take ownership of the prompt—in other words, if they can consider a way of making it more than simply an assignment, but an opportunity for them to address an issue they are passionate about to a specific audience. To help them develop this sense of audience and purpose, a discussion of exigency can be beneficial. This is one reason to talk about exigency at the beginning of the writing project. The discussion about it will differ depending on how narrowly their purpose and audience is being defined by the writing prompt, but either way, the beginning of the project is the first and probably best place to discuss exigency.

It can also be helpful to discuss exigency when students are writing their introductory paragraphs, concluding paragraphs, or as they are revising their drafts to craft a more compelling argument. These three points in the composition process are what I think of as global points, where students have an opportunity to look at the writing assignment holistically. As a reader—in and out of the classroom—the introduction and conclusion are often where I find exigent moments, and I tell students this, perhaps bringing in examples for them to review and discuss. As a writer, it's often in the middle or at the end of the writing process that I can better grasp the exigency of an argument for both myself and my readers, and this can be a point of discussion in class as well.

As my chapter asserts, asking students to think in terms of author and reader personas may also help lead to discussions on exigency. Asking students to think of personas invites them to consider what agenda or values correspond with that persona and how those considerations can help writers establish connections with their readers. Finally, exigency isn't just connected to global issues like persona, audience, and purpose; it can also be thought of in terms of templates and well-worn rhetorical moves. Showing students rhetorical patterns connected to exigency, such as how writers explain a "gap in the research," can help make it clear to students how they can articulate exigency at the sentence or passage level.

Discussion Questions

1. Can you think of any other strategies for invoking exigency other than those listed above?
2. Have you ever struggled to think of a purpose behind your writing for a particular paper? What did you do to resolve this problem?
3. What nonfiction texts have you read that made you feel the text's subject matter was absolutely essential to you?
4. Find and read an academic article, political speech, or magazine article that employs one of these strategies. Which strategy does it employ, and how effective is the text at invoking exigency?
5. What genres can you think of that are not mentioned in this article? In what ways do authors typically use exigency in those genres?

13 Assessing Source Credibility for Crafting a Well-Informed Argument

Kate Warrington, Natasha Kovalyova, and Cindy King

Overview

This article walks students through how to use critical reading strategies to help them select credible sources for their research papers and helps them understand how critical reading assignments they may have completed earlier in the semester have prepared them for the difficult task of selecting sources. Through analysis of how logos, ethos, and pathos are used in potential sources, students will understand that these persuasive techniques can influence the overall credibility of a source. Seven questions are presented that aid in critical reading, and examples of student writing are provided that demonstrate the connection between the use of persuasive techniques and their effect on the credibility of a particular source. The chapter concludes with a brief evaluation of two Internet sources on the topic of animal shelters, providing students with an anchor for evaluating sources as they prepare their own research papers.

In your writing course, you're likely to encounter a variety of assignments—reading, responding, writing essays—and each of these assignments is a building block to improved writing skills.* Research writing requires all of the skills learned in these kinds of assignments; it demands you put theory into practice, gather sources, synthesize them, and lend your voice to the ongoing conversation.

---

* This work is licensed under the Creative Commons Attribution-NonCommercial-NoDerivatives 4.0 International License (CC BY-NC-ND 4.0) and are subject to the Writing Spaces Terms of Use. To view a copy of this license, visit http://creativecommons.org/licenses/by-nc-nd/4.0/, email info@creativecommons.org, or send a letter to Creative Commons, PO Box 1866, Mountain View, CA 94042, USA. To view the Writing Spaces Terms of Use, visit http://writingspaces.org/terms-of-use.

Critical Reading for Writing

Establishing Credibility

You've probably noticed that establishing credibility (ethos) is one of the most important things an author can do, and nearly every aspect of the essay—its audience awareness, organization, and content—can affect the author's credibility. Therefore, when determining the credibility of published sources for your research paper, you'll have to be thorough and focused. Even though you may not realize it, if you have engaged in discussions or written responses to assigned readings in the past, you may already have had plenty of practice assessing an author's credibility. For example, take a look at this excerpt from Jack's reading response. Jack is responding to Dorothy Allison's essay "What Did You Expect?" that was assigned in his Composition I class:

> I feel that Dorothy Allison is a very creative and honest writer, who believes in the importance of writing about the truths of life...she doesn't have any qualms talking about where and how she was raised. Even though she is a very accomplished writer, Allison is very self conscious of how people perceive her. Her childhood seems to be the cause of her low self-esteem and inadequacies which are stated in her writing... I was happy to know that Allison decided to go with a photo shoot of her in a Laundromat. This is showing that she is a down-to-earth everyday person, which to me is more appealing than an unrealistic Barbie doll figure that a lot of famous women try to personify. In sticking to her guns about not doing the powdered sugar photo shoot, Dorothy Allison is proving that she is not a sell out, and has moral value and self worth. (Jack (pseudonym). Reader Response to "What Did You Expect?").

Jack has approached this reading assignment as an active and engaged reader. He evaluates Allison's credibility in the essay and uses examples from the text that lead him to the conclusion that "Dorothy Allison is a creative and honest writer." Jack recognizes that Allison is an "accomplished writer" who is well-educated. He learns these facts by reading the introduction to the essay that included facts about Dorothy Allison, a writer whom Jack was not familiar with before he read this essay. Jack takes this information with him as he reads the text and looks for other clues to Allison's credibility as an author. Allison's willingness to share information about her childhood, and her "down-to-earth" quality that she expresses in her writing despite her apparent fame persuades Jack that what Allison writes is genuine and important.

The qualities Jack looks for in Allison's writing to evaluate her credibility are qualities that you can use to evaluate any author's credibility. You can ask yourself:

1. Who is the author?
2. How do I know that he/she is knowledgeable about the subject?

In Jack's case, he knows who the author is because he read the introductory material, and he believes Allison is knowledgeable about the subject because she writes about herself in a way that Jack perceives to be honest and forthright. It doesn't hurt that Allison writes about herself, a topic that any reader would expect Allison to know more about than anyone else.

Determining the credibility of an author can involve more than just knowing the author's credentials and whether or not they are knowledgeable about the topic. Authors establish credibility with the way they construct their arguments. If an argument is illogical or seems to be biased in some way, this damages the author's credibility. One common mistake writers make is to represent only one side of an argument, which could make the audience believe that the author is either not knowledgeable about other possible arguments or not interested in these arguments. If an author is forthright about presenting a biased viewpoint, then you might believe the author to be more credible than one who claims to be presenting both sides of the story but does not.

Assessing Source Bias

The way authors choose to make their point is also important when evaluating sources for credibility. For example, you've probably seen the ASPCA commercials featuring melancholy music and heartbreaking pictures of sad or abused animals. The goal of these commercials is to persuade viewers to donate money to the ASPCA—and the appeal to emotions is hard to miss. The ASPCA and homeless pets have certainly benefitted from the generosity of viewers whose heartstrings were tugged by the use of emotion in these commercials.

Appealing to the reader's emotions (using pathos) can be very effective at helping the reader connect to the author's main point, but when we select sources for research projects, we must make sure that an author's appeal to emotion is not a sign of bias. Biased sources may cause readers to feel guilty about holding certain viewpoints or engaging in certain activities, which may be the goal of the source. For example, Lisa writes in her reading journal about Kasper Hauser's "Skymaul"—a parody of the SkyMall catalog that used to be found in most airlines' seatback pockets. She understands that Kasper Hauser is poking fun at consumer culture while realizing that she is an active part of that culture:

> We don't necessarily need any of the things advertised in the media or even in magazines though we more than often desire the things that might not even benefit our everyday lives… I find the pepper self-spray quite ironic; maybe it's just me but sometimes I feel like I'm actually pepper spraying myself when I purchase such things like are sold in the Skymall catalogue because maybe it just wasn't worth it or it didn't function as advertised. (Lisa (pseudonym). Reader Response to "Skymaul?").

In her response, Lisa knows that Kasper Hauser is presenting a particular side of the argument about consumer culture. Viewing the parody makes her feel a bit stupid for participating in this kind of culture—like she's "pepper spraying" herself. Kasper Hauser's "Skymaul" is biased because it only presents one side of the argument about consumerism, and it makes the reader aware of his or her place in the culture the group critiques—even causing the viewer to feel guilty or stupid for being part of that culture.

Using biased sources in your research can be problematic, particularly if you do not acknowledge that the source is biased. When you are engaging in critical reading assignments and/or evaluating sources for your research, ask yourself these questions to determine the degree to which a source is biased:

3. Is the author using emotional appeals/manipulation in his or her argument?
4. Does the author use "loaded" language to distract readers from relevant reasons and evidence?

Sometimes authors dismiss opposing arguments by claiming that these arguments are "uninformed" or "nonsensical." Some less savvy authors will be as bold as to claim another viewpoint is "stupid." Watch for these kinds of words because they are signs of bias.

Evaluating an Argument's Support

How authors put arguments together and what support they use to bolster their arguments can affect the credibility of the source. If an author makes an argument that remains logical and consistent from beginning to end, then readers are likely to be persuaded. When an author presents an illogical argument or an argument that seems to change as it develops, the author's credibility and persuasiveness is damaged. For instance, in John Freyer's "All My Life for Sale" some readers might sense that the stated purpose of the essay doesn't seem to match up with its tone. Telling his story, Freyer reflects on a project where he set up a Web site and sold all of his belongings over the Internet. He kept track of where many of his belongings went and attempted to visit his old belongings and the people who purchased them. While the reader might appreciate the author's creativity and a sense of adventure, deriving further "gains" from the initial project and publishing an essay might appear to some as merely a promotional campaign. A cautious reader might even suspect a hidden agenda behind the Freyer's project in which personal attachments were mined for money-making opportunities.

Despite Freyer's disclaimer that his motivations were more complex than just to make some money, readers who believe that his project as a whole and his essay in particular is an attempt at self-promotion will be questioning the essay with the following:

5. Is the support for the argument appropriate to the claim?
6. Are all the statements believable?
7. Is the argument consistent and complete?

Like questions 1-4, questions 5, 6, and 7 also can help you to determine whether an author is credible; these three questions address whether the argument is logically acceptable. The more logical an argument is, the more likely the reader will be persuaded.

When you evaluate a piece of writing using these seven questions, you are using critical reading and thinking skills. These are the same skills you will use when you are evaluating sources for the research essay you are preparing. You are going to want to establish your own credibility in your writing. If you use sources that aren't credible, then your own credibility will suffer.

FINDING SOURCES

While searching for sources, you will be making a lot of decisions. Some of them are easy; others are tough. Yet, regardless of what your decisions are going to be about—the focus, the argument, the support materials—at the core lies your credibility as a writer. In fact, there will be two kinds of credibility to juggle—that of your sources and that of your own. If you want to come across as a knowledgeable writer, the company you assemble (that is, the sources you bring in) will speak volumes about you and your understanding of the subject.

Striking as it might sound, credibility is not an innate quality. Credibility is established. Demonstrate a firm grasp of the matter at hand, and your audience will perceive you as a knowledgeable person, worthy of their attention. Show that you know who argues against your case, and your audience will take your argument more seriously. "But what if I am not particularly knowledgeable about the subject matter?" you might ask. "What if I am making my first scholastic steps?" Well, there is plenty of good news for you: good sources *lend you their credibility*.

How do you find good sources, then? Earlier in this chapter, we listed seven questions that can help you to determine the credibility of your sources:

1. Who is the author?
2. How do I know that he/she is knowledgeable about the subject?
3. Is the author using emotional appeals/manipulation in his or her argument?
4. Does the author use "loaded" language to distract readers from relevant reasons and evidence?
5. Is the support for the argument appropriate to the claim?
6. Are all the statements believable?
7. Is the argument consistent and complete?

These questions will help you select the sources that contribute best to your credibility as a writer. You may come across an insightful comment on your topic in a book, on a flyer, in an email, or a blog. You may hear important information in a radio program or on a late-night TV show. No media should be banned from your search effort, but you should be very picky about making the source yours. Remind yourself that sources are people and that you are about to jump into a conversation they have been having. To do so effectively, take a critical view of their conversation first. In other words, evaluate your sources.

Evaluating sources and critical reading go hand-in-hand. You read a piece critically in order to understand it. You evaluate the same piece in order to make an informed decision about "inviting" the writer to have a conversation with you on a topic. Simply put, when evaluating, you "read with an attitude" (Palmquist 49). The following advice might be useful:

> Accept nothing at face value; ask questions about your topic; look for similarities and differences in the source you read; examine the implications of what you read for your research project; be on the alert for unusual information; and note relevant sources and information. Most importantly, be open to ideas and arguments, even if you don't agree with them. Give them a chance to affect how you think about the conversation you have decided to join. (Palmquist 53)

Okay, given the variety of sources and the virtual sea of information, do you have to read and evaluate all sources in the same way? The short answer is, "It depends." The general rules of critical reading and evaluating apply to the majority of sources. However, as more and more information is posted on the Web, additional precautions are needed.

Let's revisit, for a moment, the library setting. You have probably been told that print materials collected by librarians have great advantages. They are of a high quality because librarians review and carefully select books and journals for the library to buy. Library collections are systematically organized and cataloged. In case you are having trouble navigating the collection, the library staff can help you find what you are looking for or suggest where to look.

These are all good points. But libraries and print materials do have some disadvantages. Collections are limited by the physical space and the budget. Libraries cannot buy all the books printed in the world nor can they subscribe to all periodicals out there. They specialize in some subjects, while collecting very basic materials in other fields. To find a movie that came out, say, in the early 1940s, you might need to travel to a place that holds a copy of it or use the interlibrary loan system and borrow it for a short period of time.

Don't online resources have an advantage here? Yes and no. When your computer is connected to the Internet, you have a world of information at your fingertips. Type in a search term, and hundreds, if not thousands, of documents appear on your screen in a split second. News that broke an hour ago, game schedules, flight information, stock quotes, currency exchange rates, current temperature at your location, a list of courses offered at your school next semester, a menu at a nearby restaurant—you can access all that without leaving home.

In addition to being conveniently accessible, online information comes from a variety of sources that sometimes rival those in a library. Videos, audio files, and images all reside on the Internet. Say you are writing about global warming. In addition to scholarly journal articles, news briefs, environmental agencies' reports, statistics, transcripts of Congressional hearings, activists' blogs and discussion forums, a simple Google search can also bring you videos, maps, PowerPoint presentations, and the like. To find all those resources in one library would be very difficult, if not impossible.

The Web, however, has its own disadvantages. One particularly notable concern is that because anyone can upload materials online, no one can be assured of their quality. No trained staff is out there to assist you in sieving through what you have pulled onto your screen. The sheer volume of information might be overwhelming, making you sometimes feel that there exists nothing of value on your particular topic.

There is no shortage of materials—both online and in print—as you have found by now. But which ones are good ones? To make that determination, it's time to be as picky as possible, scrutinizing the structure of their argument (logos), their motives and agendas (ethos), and their fair use of emotional appeals (pathos).

When you are writing a research paper, you will be expected to do precisely that, and more. You will also need to enter in a conversation with your sources and respond to them rather than report what they are saying. While your audience will, no doubt, benefit from knowing what experts have said, they are reading your paper and are interested in hearing what you have to say. Listen to what your sources say (that is, *read* carefully and critically) and try to understand their position. Then, agree or disagree, draw parallels between their views and yours, ask questions and take sides. Translated onto a written page, your conversation will take the shape of your quoting, paraphrasing, and summarizing. By doing so, you will be contributing to the discussion with your own observations, questions, comments, and concerns.

Selecting Sources Sample Topic: Animal Treatment

Let's explore the topic of animal treatment. After watching an ASPCA commercial, you decided to explore the topic of animal shelters. Your interest in the topic was piqued by a brief memory of a handmade poster you saw earlier at a gas station. "Emily Missing," you remember it saying. Judging by the picture, Emily happened to be a kitten that ran away. "What if someone found Emily but had not seen the poster?" you wondered. Someone could have tried to return her to her owners if she wore a tag, or Emily could have been turned in to the nearest animal shelter or humane society. With Emily's fortune at the back of your mind, you want to learn more about animals in animal shelters and possibly write your findings in a paper.

You have a zillion questions to ask. How many animal shelters are currently in operation in the United States, or even in a given state? How many animals are kept there? What are the most common animals in a shelter? Do most animals in shelters get adopted? How do shelters ensure that an animal goes to good hands and not to abusive owners or research labs? What happens to those who cannot find a new owner because of their age, illness, or behavioral problems? How do shelters raise money? What happens to animals when a shelter cannot house them any longer?

Following in the steps of dozens of your fellow classmates, you opened a Google search and typed in "animal shelter" (see figure 1). Among the top results, you saw links to your local animal shelters and other rescue organizations.

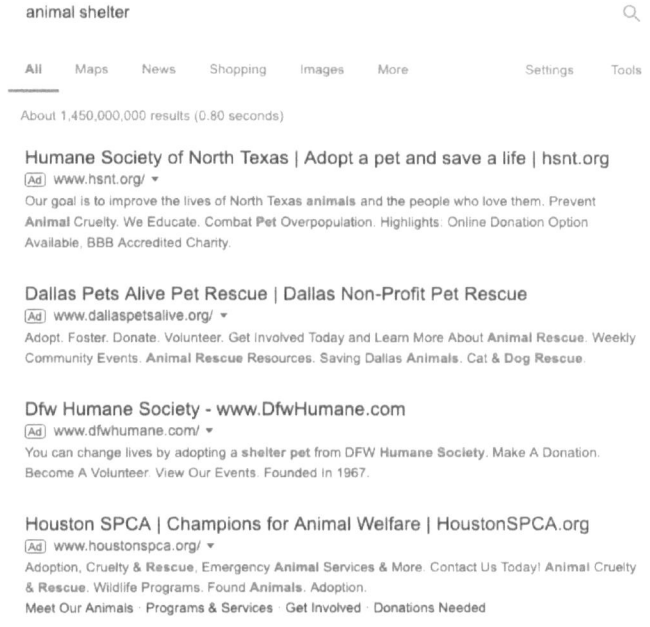

Figure 1. Google search for "animal shelter" shows several ad results, including "Humane Society of North Texas," "Dallas Pets Alive Pet Rescue," DFW Humane Society," and "Houston SPCA."

When searching for "animal shelter," you receive more than one billion results. You are now faced with a formidable evaluation task, but you can't possibly look at all of these sources. You could choose to narrow your search terms to something like "animal shelters and lost pets" (which yields 66,200,000 results) or take Google's apparent suggestion and focus your search on animal shelters in your local area. Let's say you decide to focus on the Humane Society of North Texas, the first result from your original search (see figure 2).

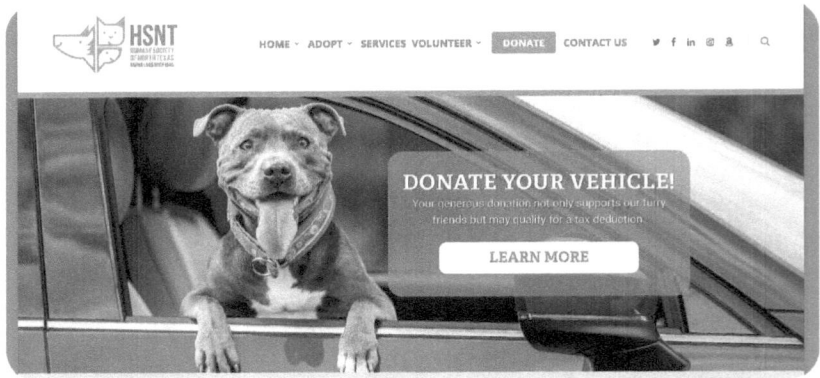

Figure 2. The Humane Society of North Texas homepage shows the organization's logo, a basic navigational menu, and a photo of a large dog looking out a car window into the camera. Text next to the dog encourages viewers to donate their vehicle in support of the Humane Society.

To guide you during this evaluation process are the critical reading questions that we discussed earlier.

1. Who is the author?
2. How do I know that he/she is knowledgeable about the subject?
3. Is the author using emotional appeals/manipulation in his or her argument?
4. Does the author use "loaded" language to distract readers from relevant reasons and evidence?
5. Is the support for the argument appropriate to the claim?
6. Are all the statements believable?
7. Is the argument consistent and complete?

Using the Questions to Determine Credibility

Just by looking at the homepage, it is clear that the Humane Society of North Texas sponsors and maintains the site. After clicking on some of the more specific links on the top of the page, you locate some press releases that name individual authors and their titles. For example, if you clicked on the item "Newsroom" from the drop-down menu under "Home," then on the press release titled "We Like Big Mutts and We Cannot Lie (Ok-Cats, Too)!," you will be directed to the page shown here in Figure 3. Notice that the author is Cassie Lackey, who is the Director of Communications for the Humane Society of North Texas. Because Lackey works for the Humane Society of North Texas, she likely has access to accurate information about this organization. Her role as Director of Communications is to inform the community about news related to the Humane Society, so from what we can tell so far, she appears to be a credible author (see figure 3).

Cassie Lackey
Director of Communications
Humane Society of North Texas
Cell: 817-909-0667
Email: communications@hsnt.org

FOR IMMEDIATE RELEASE

We Like Big Mutts and We Cannot Lie (Ok–Cats, Too)!

Fort Worth, Texas, May 24, 2019:
The Humane Society of North Texas (HSNT), will fly over 160 dogs and cats on Saturday, May 25, 2019, to Washington and Idaho. HSNT is partnering with Wings of Rescue, GreaterGood.org, and the ASPCA® (The American Society for the Prevention of Cruelty to Animals®) to fly pets to the Pacific Northwest, where adopters are excitedly awaiting big and small furry friends alike! Flying large dogs to other states will ease overcrowding in HSNT's shelter.

Large dogs are surrendered to HSNT consistently and abundantly. What HSNT has recognized is the majority of large dogs coming through its doors are much harder to adopt into homes due to their size. Larger dogs are susceptible to spending longer times in the shelter waiting for their forever homes. There is a tremendous need for adopters and fosters of large dogs. To learn more about the available pets at the Humane Society of North Texas, visit hsnt.org.

"The Humane Society of North Texas is beyond grateful for these lifesaving flights. We desperately need to find homes for our larger dogs," said Cassie Lackey, Director of Communications at HSNT. "As our intake continues to grow, we need to pursue finding forever homes and placement for the voiceless pets in our care."

Figure 3. "We Like Big Mutts and We Cannot Lie (Ok-Cats, Too)!" press release was found by following the "Newsroom" link from hsnt.org. The release discusses a partnership with several organizations that will allow them to fly larger dogs to other states to be adopted, thus increasing rates of adoption. Source: The Human Society of North Texas.

While it appears as if this source has a credible author, we should look for other clues to help us feel certain about its credibility. The extension .org in the URL indicates that this Web site is not set up for commercial purposes—that is, not for deriving profit from the activity on the site. In fact, the central features of the site are the menu items at the top of the home page: Adopt, Services Volunteer, and Donate. The information appears very straightforward and oriented toward a clear purpose: to help people adopt animals or volunteer their time and money to help homeless animals.

By now, it's easy to conclude that *hsnt.org* may be a useful source if you live in the North Texas area and want to focus your research on local animal shelters. But, you can't hang your hat on just one source.

After browsing through several local animal shelter sites, you expand your search and click on the Web site for the People for the Ethical Treatment of Animals (PETA): www.peta.org. The banner has a direct slogan: "Animals are not ours to experiment on, eat, wear, use for entertainment, or abuse in any other way." That slogan provides some insight into the mission of the organization. The breadth and depth of information you find here is impressive: feature stories, news briefs, files on a series of animal cruelty issues, factsheets, blog posts, and a sizeable collection of videos. It is here, however, that a peculiar approach to presenting information becomes prominent, namely, the extensive use of celebrities to attract attention and (hopefully) advance the organization's cause.

You might also notice that on this site a lot of effort is put into raising awareness about animal cruelty and stirring grassroots activism. You will find tips for activists, templates of correspondence to send to public officials, and news of upcoming events. Does that constitute a bias? Well, it definitely points to a well-shaped agenda, and you need to recognize that, whether you agree or disagree with the mission the site is promoting. Without doubt, some of the material you come across can be considered controversial. Therefore, when you consider the question, "Are all the statements believable?" think not only about your own assessment of the material but also about what your audience may think. If your audience believes that some of the source material you choose to include in your paper is not believable, then your credibility will be damaged. After carefully evaluating PETA's Web site, you will likely decide that while it contains some useful and credible information, you will need to use this site with care and acknowledge its agenda.

All information that you have discovered so far is valuable, but you know that to write a well-informed research paper, you'll have to search further.

Conclusion

To succeed as a researcher, and ultimately a persuasive, credible writer, you have learned that you can't fly solo—that, in fact, no one can go it alone. You will come to understand that strong, well-defended arguments need support, just as, for instance, most singers need a solid back-up band. And like any good front person, you should audition and choose carefully those who will stand behind you. In other words, interrogate those sources. Ask the tough questions. If you do so, you can resist the charges of loaded language, recognize when sources tug at your heartstrings, and leave unreliable statements behind.

This chapter has taken you step-by-step through the process of how to critically evaluate your sources. With practice, this type of thinking will become a natural part of your approach to both assigned reading and research material as well to what's outside the classroom. And the more critical you are in your reading and research, the more it will become a part of how you view the world, be it in the classroom, online, or virtually everywhere. This ability to encounter the world with a critical eye is a valuable tool, one that allows you to more fully engage with it. And your capacity for determining credibility can help you make informed decisions in your writing, work, and life.

Works Cited

Allison, Dorothy. "What Did You Expect?" Atwan, pp. 588-594.
Atwan, Robert. *Convergences*. 3rd ed., Bedford/St. Martin's, 2009.
Freyer, John. "All My Life For Sale." Atwan, pp. 80-92.
Hauser, Kasper. "Skymaul." Atwan, pp. 560-561.
Humane Society of North Texas, 2019, Hsnt.org. Accessed 28 May 2019.
Lisa (pseudonym). "Reader response to 'Skymaul.'" *University of North Texas Dallas*, November 3, 2010. Electronic posting on class discussion board.
Jack (pseudonym). "Reader response to 'What did you Expect.'" *University of North Texas Dallas*, September 29, 2010. Electronic posting on class discussion board.
Palmquist, Mike. *The Bedford Researcher*. 3rd ed., Bedford/St Martin's, 2009.
People for the Ethical Treatment of Animals, 2019, peta.org. Accessed 28 May 2019.

Teacher Resources for Assessing Source Credibility for Crafting a Well-Informed Argument by Kate Warrington, Natasha Kovalyova, and Cindy King

Overview and Teaching Strategies

This essay is ideally taught in preparation for collecting sources for research writing and provides a nice scaffold for students who have already engaged in some critical reading assignments or reading responses prior to being assigned a research writing assignment. The flow of activities was designed to support students in introductory composition, although the topic of source evaluation fits well at all levels, across the curriculum. Recognizing a widespread practice among college students to Google their topics, we have found it critical to introduce students to some concrete ways to evaluate all types of sources since we've found it to be unlikely (and impractical) to prohibit the use of Web sources.

Questions

1. How, if at all, do sources dealing with certain subjects and/or arguments call for a more rigorous scrutiny of credibility? For example, do those that are emotionally charged demand a closer look? Do sources in highly specialized fields require you to scrutinize the structure of their arguments more carefully?
2. To what extent should you consider an author's credentials when determining his or her knowledge of the field, and ultimately the credibility of the source? When, for example, might a source written by a layperson be as valuable as one by an expert in the field? How might you compare, for instance, an article on juvenile delinquency written by a legislator to one produced by a social psychologist? How might you treat a book written by a physician who is also a TV personality?
3. Do certain subjects, purposes, and audiences allow for a less critical evaluation of bias? How, specifically, might you determine when sources use emotional appeals without bias?
4. What further challenges do Internet sources pose when it comes to gauging their credibility? How, for example, can you evaluate

credibility when a Web site's content comes from an indeterminate source or multiple authors?
5. In what situations, if any, might you disregard credibility of a source? If a source lacks credibility according to your examination through critical reading, does it always mean you shouldn't use it? How, if at all, might you use a source that lacks credibility in your essay?

Activities

The following are two class activities that can help students put to action the advice and steps for critical reading discussed in the essay.

Critical Reading Practice

To get students more comfortable with reading academic writing, have them practice these skills in small groups in a low-stakes environment. Hand out a short scholarly source (3 to 5 pages) on an accessible topic and give them time in class to read it. Then divide them into small groups and ask them to apply the seven questions presented in the essay to this source. Once they have done so, they present to the class their recommendation about whether the source is credible, and if they would or wouldn't use it in their research paper. These presentations typically generate a vibrant class discussion.

Web source Evaluation Practice

Since most students feel comfortable using the popular Internet to find sources for their research, offer them an opportunity to work through credibility of Internet sources during small group work in class. Ask each small group to choose a topic (it can be a topic they plan to work with for their research paper) and conduct an Internet search for sources on that topic. Once they have located a source that they believe looks like it has good information, ask them to locate basic information like the author/sponsoring organization and publication date. In many cases, this information will be difficult to locate, which not only helps them to prepare for the challenges they may face citing Internet sources, but also helps them to take a second look at the credibility of Internet sources.

Contributors

Kevin Cassell teaches for the Writing Program in the Department of English at the University of Arizona. In addition to teaching Foundations Writing courses for both domestic and international students, he currently coordinates the Writing Program's upper-division curriculum in business and technical writing. Some of his interests include curriculum design using multilayered simulation-based practicums, discipline-based writing (WID/WAC) through the lens of user experience (UX), apprehending the rhetorical effects of text conventions through multisensory reading strategies, and adaptive interface technologies for the visually impaired.

Jenae Cohn is Academic Technology Specialist in the Program in Writing and Rhetoric at Stanford University, where she supports students and instructors in incorporating critical digital pedagogy into the teaching of writing. She has published in *Computers and Composition, Transformative Dialogues,* and *Kairos.*

Ron DePeter is Professor of English, and Writing Center Director, at Delaware Valley University in Doylestown, Pennsylvania. He teaches first year and upper level composition courses and themed courses such as Writing about Animals and Themes in Country Music. Ron has previously published essays on teaching and writing in *The Practice of Response, Elements of Alternate Style,* and *Writing on the Edge.*

William FitzGerald is Associate Professor of English at Rutgers-University Camden, where he directs the First Year Writing Program. He is author of *Spiritual Modalities: Prayer as Rhetoric and Performance* and co-author of *The Craft of Research, 4e*. His research interests include the pedagogy of style and research-based writing and appear in a range of edited collections.

Melanie Gagich is Associate College Lecturer at Cleveland State University, where she teaches first-year writing and an upper-level composition course focused on writing and new media. She has published in the *Journal of Interactive Technology* and *Pedagogy* and co-authored the open access textbook, *A Guide to Rhetoric, Genre, and Success in First-Year Writing.*

Craig Hulst is Senior Affiliate Professor at Grand Valley State University, where he teaches First-year Writing. He is also a contributing editor for the journal *Chinese Literature and Culture.*

Contributors

Cindy King is Assistant Professor of English at Dixie State University, where she teaches creative writing, composition, and print journal publication. Her poetry has appeared in *The Sun, Prairie Schooner, Gettysburg Review*, and elsewhere. She is the author of a poetry chapbook, *Easy Street* (Dancing Girl Press) and *Zoonotic* (Tinder Box Editions).

Natalia Kovalyova (iSchool, UT Austin) studies the relationships between discourse and power in a variety of contexts from presidential communication to academic writing. Her most recent research focuses on archival practices in organizations and government agencies and aims at documenting and understanding the enduring practices of control over public memory, group identities, and knowledge making. She is a member of the National Communication Association and Rhetoric Society of America.

Dan Melzer is Associate Professor of Rhetoric and Composition at the University of California, Davis, where he directs the First-Year Composition program and teaches first-year composition and graduate composition theory and practice courses. He has published the book *Assignments Across the Curriculum* and is a co-author of the book *Sustainable WAC*, and his articles have appeared in *CCCC, WPA, The WAC Journal*, and *JBW*.

Craig A. Meyer is Assistant Professor at Texas A&M University – Kingsville. His research interests include histories of rhetoric, composition theory and practice, social justice, disability studies, and ethos. He has published work with *CCCC-IP, Moon City Press, The Chronicle of Higher Education*, and various book collections (mostly connecting Star Trek to his research areas).

Kathleen J. Ryan is Associate Professor of Rhetoric and Writing at Montana State University. She is a coeditor of *Rethinking Ethos: A Feminist Ecological Approach to Rhetoric*, a coauthor of *GenAdmin: Theorizing WPA Identities in the Twenty-First Century*, and coeditor of *Walking and Talking Feminist Rhetorics: Landmark Essays and Controversies*. In addition, she has articles in a range of writing and rhetoric journals on feminist rhetorics and writing program administration.

Kirk St.Amant is Professor and Eunice C. Williamson Endowed Chair in Technical Communication and Research Faculty Member with the Center for Biomedical Engineering and Rehabilitation Science (CBERS) at Louisiana Tech University. Kirk also serves as the Director of Tech's Usability Studies Research Center and its Health and Medical Communication Research Center. He holds appointments as an Adjunct Professor of International Health and Medical Communication with the University of Limerick (Ireland), a Guest Professor of Usability Studies with Southeast University (China), and a Research Fellow and Adjunct Professor of User Experience Design with the University of Strasbourg (France).

Marjorie Stewart is Associate Professor of English at Glenville State College in West Virginia. She teaches corequisite first year composition, journalism, and creative nonfiction. She is the art advisor for *The Trillium*, the college literary magazine, and writes plays performed by the theater program.She is a published poet and essayist and has 25 play productions, primarily in the Pittsburgh area.

Quentin Vieregge is Associate Professor of English at Universtity of Wisconsin-Eau Claire—Barron County. He teaches composition, literature, business communication, and film courses. He has published in the fields of popular culture and rhetoric and composition. He is the co-author of two books: *Agency in the Age of Peer Production* and *The United States Constitution in Film: Part of Our National Culture*.

Kate Warrington is Director of General Education at Western Governors University where she is engaged in reinventing liberal studies in a fully online, competency-based environment that focuses on student success. Her scholarly work has appeared in *Praxis: A Writing Center Journal*, *The Writing Center Journal*, and in several edited collections.

About the Editors

Dr. Dana Driscoll is Professor of English at Indiana University of Pennsylvania, where she teaches in the Composition and Applied Linguistics graduate program and directs the Jones White Writing Center. Her scholarly interests include composition pedagogy, writing centers, writing transfer and writerly development, research methodologies, writing across the curriculum, and assessment.

Dr. Mary Stewart is Assistant Professor and the Assessment Coordinator for the English Department at Indiana University of Pennsylvania. Her research, which is primarily qualitative, focuses on collaborative and interactive learning, blended and online writing instruction, composition pedagogy, and teaching with technology.

Dr. Matthew Vetter is Assistant Professor of English at Indiana University of Pennsylvania and affiliate faculty in the Composition and Applied Linguistics PhD Program. A scholar in writing, rhetoric, and digital humanities, his research explores how technologies shape writing and writing pedagogy.